OUT OF THE BOX

Out of the Box

A Memoir

Written by:
DuBonna L. Dawkins

Copyright © 2025 Dubonna Dawkins
All Scripture quotations within are from the Kings James version
All rights reserved.
Published in the United States
Empowerment Zone Publishing
Cincinnati, OH

EIN: 978-0-9789761-5-6

DEDICATION

I dedicate this story of my deliverance, from the spirit that repeatedly kept me in boxes throughout the majority of my life, to all those who prayed for me, wiped my tears and simply listened. I know that there were times in my life when I made wrong choices, but I also know that through all those difficult circumstances, the prayers my mom sent up for me went through to Heaven, and the pride I saw in my father's eyes, kept me from straying too far away. For never giving up on me when I was young and rebellious, and for loving me, I thank you both. Today, even after your deaths, I am honored to call you two of my very best friends in the world. Through my depression as a young wife and mother, I know the strength of my husband and love from my children kept me from death, and allow me to tell my story today. Thank you for showing me what family means. And most importantly, I give God and my Lord and Savior Jesus Christ, all the honor, praise, and glory for His wonderous grace and mercy. Every day, I continue to choose.

CONTENTS

Introduction		viii
1	What is a Box	1
2	The Anatomy of a Box	3
3	The Box Effect	11
4	The Cost of Confinement	14
5	Edges that Pulled Me In	16
6	Drifting into the Dim	23
7	The Lure of the Lessor Space	26
8	When the Walls Start Whispering	29
9	Bound by Accident	32
10	The Capture	39
11	The Unnoticed Descent	49
12	Constructing Boarders	62
13	The Quiet Pull into Small Spaces	68
14	About the Box	73
15	The Early Days	77

16	Testing the Waters	91
17	Shattered Glass	101
18	Growing into Her	118
19	My Journey to the Upper Room	125
20	The Test	132
21	The Breaking Point	145
22	A Wound not Easily Healed	163
23	The Day I Didn't Push Through	173
24	A Fresh Beginning	179
25	Grace in the Growing	184

OUT OF THE BOX

INTRODUCTION

Where do I begin? Even today, as I look back over my life, I cannot pinpoint an exact day when I got trapped in the box, or the day I realized I was trapped, nor what box it was—number one, five, seven—I hadn't started counting. Somehow, I found myself going from box to box—whether I stepped in, jumped in, stumbled in or was shoved in, I was there—in darkness, feeling alone, sad, angry and guilty. I was unsure of what I could have done differently, what I should have said, done, revealed, or exposed. There were moments when I knew I was no longer myself, but a robot—some fabrication of what I used to be—or at least what I knew in my heart, I truly was. I acted on the commands I heard from outside of myself, most times, unaware of where those sounds originated and why I heard them, and why they were so faint and difficult to really comprehend. I think the boxes gradually surrounded me, little by little, and before I knew it, I was crying before the Lord, "Please help me; I can't stand it anymore, I want out!" I loved, I hated, I regretted, I learned, I grew.

I remember the day I looked closely at my life and for the first time realized I had let go of my calling, my mission. Although I wasn't entirely sure what my mission was—my purpose, I knew that there was a greater plan God had for me and I yearned to make steps towards fulfilling it. Life was complicated, too complicated. My priorities were all mixed up, and what should have been put first in my life was not first. At least for me, not in the order that I believe God intended for it to be, nor in the order I had imagined it to be. But even worse than that, I felt trapped with no way out. I felt like I was trying to make things happen myself. I was not operating in my gift or my calling. As a child, I had plans for my life, dreams I wanted to fulfill, goals to accomplish, and a sincere belief that life is good, people are good, and if you love God, do what's right, be kind to others, no dream is unreachable. Someone, I had lost sight of my purpose, consumed by man's ideologies, the world's concept of what is normal, acceptable, right—forsaking God's Word and wandering into wildernesses where I knew God was present, but not pleased.

God always makes a way of escape, but I wasn't certain if the Lord wanted me to escape quietly and peaceably, or to bust out of the box and never look back. Finally, I was tired of being disobedient! I finally realized that I couldn't continue to blame others for my behavior. No matter what happened to me, or what others had done to me, I had a choice and I decided to choose God. I had strayed away from Him, returned like the prodigal son—or daughter in my case; forsaken what I had known to be right, then finally leaned again towards the only source of true Joy—Jesus!

I know some of you reading this book may not look to Jesus as your only true source of joy. My intention is not to convince anyone what to believe, who to believe or in whom, or how to believe, but to make a choice. In the twenty-fourth chapter of the book of Joshua of the Holy Bible, Joshua gathers the tribes of Israel and calls for the elders to present themselves before God. Joshua begins to remind them how the God of Abraham had led them through the land of Canaan, brought their fathers out of Egypt, took them over Jordan to Jericho, gave them land they hadn't worked for, and vineyards they hadn't planted. Joshua asked them if it seemed evil to serve the Lord, even after everything He had done for them; he told them to choose who they would serve. He then goes on to say, "As for me and my house, I will serve the Lord" (Joshua 24:15).

Some might say, "That's a great story." I've heard many who believe that the Bible is merely a history book or a collection of figurative short stories, metaphors, poems and prose. Whether you believe the Bible to be the Word of God, inspired by God, or a historical document, I ask you to keep an open mind, as I use biblical stories and scientific data to share examples of *"Out of the Box"* scenarios.

1 WHAT IS A BOX

When I first realized I was in a box, unsure of what to do, not able to hear God's voice, I decided to just stand, and stand I did. I stood until every ounce of strength was removed from my frail, and weak body. Then God stepped in, extended His hand and pulled me out. The scariest part of it was that the very box that I found to be so devastating, was nothing compared to the series of boxes that followed. But it wasn't until I realized that my entire life was full of "out of the box" experiences that I was able to overcome. And overcoming meant, being willing to step up to the challenge. It meant, being prepared to fight, and fight until the end. It meant, facing my own shortcomings and embracing humility. It meant, loving God and putting Him first in all aspects of my life and following his lead while not knowing where I would end up.

The American Heritage dictionary defines a Box as "A rectangular container typically having a lid or cover." Another meaning is "An awkward or perplexing situation; predicament." With this being stated, I am therefore defining a box as any situation or circumstance that is uneasy, where you feel held inside or trapped. You are bound and restricted and held within specific boundaries. When you look up, there's a wall. When you look down, there's a wall. There is a wall in the front of you and behind you, and finally walls on the right and left of you. The feelings you feel while inside the box bring stress, anxiety or worry. But like situations or circumstances where we feel trapped, isolated or separated from the world, loved ones, friends—stuck within our own thoughts, memories, painful experiences, they are different, and most time unique, just like boxes.

2 THE ANATOMY OF A BOX

Let's look at the various types of materials boxes can be made of—what I call *The Anatomy*. First, let me explain that although I am referring to physical properties when looking at boxes. These physical characteristics actually represent different things for different people. For some, a box may be a bad habit, for others—a stronghold; a box for others may be a relationship, a situation you don't know how to escape from, or even the result of a bad decision. And for some, a box may be a fear, a regret, or even guilt. We all have different things that keep, or have kept us bound, influence our decisions, tempt our senses and shift our focus. Therefore, we have to examine our own lives, work to understand our individual struggles, learn to identify them, study to overcome them and move forward, remembering to make different decisions when we're faced with those struggles again.

There's a line in a song by Jonathan McReynolds that says, "The Devil, he learns from our mistakes." The song goes on to suggest that even when we don't learn from our mistakes, the Devil does, and that's why we keep making the same mistakes over and over again. Have you ever noticed how we keep making the same mistakes over and over again? We ask for forgiveness, promising ourselves we'll do better — and then, before we know it, we fall right back into the same patterns. We say we're going to cut down on sugar, but then someone at work brings in a chocolate cake. We vow to be more patient in traffic, but the moment someone cuts us off, we're ready to explode. Or we decide to take a break from social media, but as soon as we wake up, our fingers automatically open Facebook.

We all have different internal struggles. What challenges one person might have, may not faze another. But that's exactly how the enemy works. He studies our habits, learns our weaknesses, and uses then to keep us trapped in the same cycles—sometimes leaving us stuck in a box we don't know how to escape from. Just as our challenges are different, so are our boxes. Their compositions vary—some are thin and easy to tear through, while others are thick, reinforced, and nearly impossible to break. The strength and difficulty of freeing ourselves often depend on what those boxes are made of. **When I think about box materials, they can range from notebook paper, construction paper, cardboard, wood panelling, plywood, tin, metal, and even steel, just to name a few. I'm sure while reading this you can identify hundreds of other potential materials you can construct a box with.**

Let's look at what some might consider the weakest material a box can be made of—notebook paper. As a child, I made boxes using notebook paper and tape. Now imagine yourself physically being inside a box made of notebook paper. I would argue that it would be relatively easy to escape from this box. A simple punch with the fist would most likely break the paper, and any adult, teen or young child would be able to free him/herself without the feeling of panic or anxiety.

Now imagine a newborn infant placed in that same box made of notebook paper. Would that infant have the ability to escape? No, not intentionally. First, infants have no understanding of who they are or where they are in the world. Second, they don't know they're not supposed to be in a box. Third, they have no awareness of Newton's Law of Motion, which states, an object at rest remains at rest, and an object in motion remains in motion at a constant speed and in a straight line unless acted upon by an unbalanced force. The acceleration of an object depends on the amount of force applied. Yet, infants naturally move — they kick their legs and wave their arms — and, in time, that simple, instinctive motion might be enough to tear through the paper.

Now, when I think about one of my grandsons, who is five years old, if I were to ask him, "What is Newton's Law of Motion?" he would probably raise his eyebrows the way he does when something doesn't make sense and say, "I don't know." He might even give me that look that says, "Are you serious, Ammah? How would I know that?" But even though he doesn't know the definition — and truthfully, many adults don't either — if we were playing a game and I placed him in a box made of notebook paper, he would instinctively know that if he punched or kicked hard enough, he could break free with little effort. His heart might beat a bit faster from the excitement, but being enclosed in that paper box wouldn't fill him with panic or anxiety. In fact, once he escaped, he'd probably laugh and ask, "Can we do it again?"

For a moment, let's imagine we're inside a box made of cardboard. Regardless of how we got there—the fact remains, we're there. We have no tools to help us escape except our physical body, our mind, our senses, our knowledge, or our past lived experiences. My five-year-old grandson, my nine-year-old granddaughter, and even my ten-year-old grandson may not yet have the deductive or inductive reasoning skills needed to figure out how to get out of that cardboard box. For the sake of clarity, *deductive reasoning* is a logical approach that moves from general ideas to specific conclusions. It's often contrasted with *inductive reasoning*, which starts with specific observations and leads to broader generalizations or conclusions.

Stated another way, children may not be able to deduct how to get out of a situation or induce how because of lack of knowledge or experiences. Now, my 10-year-old grandson would be so determined to escape from that box, that he may kick the box to the point of exhaustion, but I'm still not certain he would be able to escape.

As adults, we possess both deductive and inductive reasoning. We've gained knowledge, developed logic, and accumulated enough experience to recognize that a cardboard box isn't a permanent barrier. Yet, many of us remain trapped inside boxes of our own making — boxes built not of cardboard, but of fear, doubt, disappointment, and pain. Unlike children, who act instinctively and push against limitations, we sometimes overthink our way into staying confined. We analyze the walls, question the structure, and convince ourselves the box is stronger than it really is.

For me, I've never been physically trapped in a cardboard box, although I have found memories of playing with refrigerator boxes as a young child, after the delivery of a new refrigerator. However, I have an understanding from past experience that if cardboard gets wet, it's easy to tear and poke holes in. Without having any physical tools, if I were placed in a cardboard box, I can imagine using my own saliva to moisten the cardboard, and eventually—layer by layer—work my way out. Although it would take more effort to escape from a cardboard box then a box made of notebook paper, I'm confident I could escape with minimal fear and worry.

If we look at this is terms of situational boxes, opposed to physical boxes. There are certain situations we may find it easier to escape from, resist, or forgive ourselves of, because we have past experience, memories and knowledge to pull from on how we overcame that situation in the past. There are times when we may have been able to use our own resources, whether mental strength, physical attributes, logic or reasoning when facing difficult challenges, but what do we do when our own resources aren't enough?

As we move on, let's consider wooden, tin, metal and steel boxes. In the physical, I would propose to you that it would be extremely difficult, or maybe even impossible to escape from a box made of wood that had been nailed together; or a box made of metal, tin, or steel that had been soldered together, without any tools. Now when I say tin, I am not referring to tin foil.

In high school, I remember taking home economics and industrial arts. In industrial arts, I recall making a jewelry box that I soldered myself, with the help of my teacher of course. I also remember observing my dad soldering pipes and faucets in the basement. I remember him wearing goggles and seeing the sparks fly from the soldering gun and witnessed the heat fuse the objects together. While writing this book I asked Google, "What is the strongest way of joining 2 pieces of steel together?" Here's the answer I got, "How Welding Works. Welding joins metals by melting and fusing them together, typically with the addition of a welding filler metal. The joints produced are strong – usually as strong as the metals joined, or even stronger. To fuse the metals, you apply a concentrated heat directly to the joint area."

What stood out to me is the line that says, the joints produced are strong – usually as strong as the metals joined, or **even stronger.** This tells me that the joints produced to keep the box closed are even stronger than the actual box itself. What does this mean in terms of life's boxes? I found myself in many boxes over the course of my life. Some boxes surrounded me as early as elementary school. Even though at the time, I had no idea I was in a box. In reading this book, you may also realize that you have also been in boxes—walking in some, being pushed in some, tricked in some, or even realizing you were born in one. But what I've learned, and am still learning, is that the fears that invade our heart, and thoughts that intrude our mind, become the joints that keep us bound and are even stronger than the attributes of the boxes that bind us.

Now as I reflect back, when I found myself in the boxes made of the strongest steel, my physical strength, experiences, knowledge and reasoning were never enough. I needed tools with me—tools that were a part of me, with me and within me—to escape those boxes. I learned that the tools I needed were my armour.

> **Finally, my brethren, be strong in the Lord, and in the power of his might. Put on the whole amour of God, that ye may be able to stand against the wiles of the devil. For we wrestle not against flesh and blood, but against principalities, against powers, against the rulers of the darkness of this world, against spiritual wickedness in high places. Wherefore take unto you the whole amour of**

God, that ye may be able to withstand in the evil day, and having done all, to stand. Stand therefore, having your loins girt about with truth, and having on the breastplate of righteousness; And your feet shod with the preparation of the gospel of peace; Above all, taking the shield of faith, wherewith ye shall be able to quench all the fiery darts of the wicked. And take the helmet of salvation, and the sword of the Spirit, which is the word of God. (Ephesians: 6:10 – 17).

For me, it was knowing the truth, walking in righteousness, having the peace that surpasses all understanding, holding onto faith, and finding comfort in the assurance of salvation. Most importantly, it was keeping my sword — the Word — hidden in my heart. These became the very things that equipped me to break free and be delivered from boxes far stronger than paper or cardboard — boxes made of steel. But breaking free isn't a one-time event. It's an ongoing process — learning to recognize when you're in a box, identifying the steps needed to escape, and faithfully using the armor you've been given. It's not enough to simply have the armor; you must also understand how to use each piece.

OUT OF THE BOX

3 THE BOX EFFECT

Now, let's take a closer look at the effects that being bound inside a box can have on our lives. Keep in mind, these are physical illustrations that represent deeper **spiritual, emotional, social** and **psychological** strongholds.

First, a box keeps you *bound*.
Can you imagine being placed in a wooden box, unable to stretch your arms or legs — confined, with only limited movement and mobility?

Second, a box *suffocates* you.
Picture losing oxygen, second by second, fully aware that your final breath is approaching. Images of your life race through your imagination until endless sleep overtakes you.

Third, a box *limits your potential.*
Close your eyes and see yourself inside that wooden box, dreaming of what you could be doing if you weren't trapped there — meeting your soulmate, graduating from college, landing that C-suite position, starting your own business, holding your baby or grandbaby, traveling

to Belize, Paris, or Amsterdam. Then realize those are only dreams, fading away like mist until they disappear completely.

Fourth, a box makes you *feel helpless*.
Envision pounding on the wooden walls until your knuckles bleed and your skin begins to tear. You have no sword to pierce the plywood, no faith that someone will come to rescue you.

Fifth, a box *prevents others from reaching you*.
Imagine being sealed inside a steel box, hearing the cries of your loved ones — wondering where you are, why you've forsaken them, why they can't hear your voice.

Sixth, a box *prevents you from reaching others*.
Visualize yourself wailing, pounding, screaming for help, but no one can hear you. Imagine losing your voice after long days and nights of crying out, until you can no longer even whisper, *"Help me."*

Seventh, a box keeps you from *hearing* what's outside.
Picture yourself wondering what the world looks like beyond those walls. What are your loved ones doing and saying? Imagine never again hearing birds sing, waves crash, an infant cry, or your favorite song.

Eighth, a box keeps you *focused only on what's inside*.
Can you imagine staring into constant darkness — forever?

Ninth, a box can also be a *place of protection*.
Consider being separated from the outside world, believing it would lead to death — yet later realizing that, in truth, that box was your shield. Once set free, you appreciate that confinement was for your preservation.

Tenth, a box can become a *place of solitude and reflection*.
Think of the loneliness — feeling abandoned by family and friends — yet when you finally emerge, you discover renewed strength, clarity, and purpose. The separation was necessary. It was essential for your survival and calling.

Finally, a box doesn't only affect the one inside; *it impacts those outside as well.*
Reflect on the broken hearts of loved ones who've lost connection with you. Consider how your absence reshapes their paths, how their destinies bend because of your absence.

How does someone get into a box?

I'm certain there are numerous ways to get trapped in a box. But we are going to discuss nine ways I've learned we find ourselves in boxes.

1. Unknowingly walking into the box
2. Being drawn into the box
3. Being tricked into getting into the box
4. Knowingly and willfully walking into the box
5. Jumping into the box with the intention of jumping back out
6. Being pushed into the box against your will
7. Unknowingly placed in a box
8. Building our own box and stepping into it
9. Life builds a box around you

4 THE COSTS OF CONFINEMENT

There is always a cost to living inside a box—not a box made of wood or cardboard, but a box built quietly over time, from moments that broke us, words that wounded us, and needs that went unmet. At first, the box feels like protection, a shield, a place to hide what hurts. It feels like a place where disappointment can't find us again—a place where no one can touch what's still tender. But over time, the box begins to cost us more than it protects us. Inside the box, you can't stretch, you can't grow and you can't breathe deeply. Every movement is small, cautious, controlled. You start to believe that this cramped space is all you deserve—all you're capable of.

Inside the box, your voice gets quieter. Your confidence shrinks. Your dreams stop reaching beyond the walls. Anger builds because you know you were made for more, but you feel trapped by what happened to you and by what *should* have happened but didn't. Inside the box, relationships suffer. People want to get close, but you've learned that closeness can be dangerous. So, you keep everyone at arm's length—not because you don't care, but because caring once cost you too much. Inside the box, purpose fades. You stop taking risks. You stop showing up boldly. You settle, not because you want to, but because the walls of your own pain whisper, *"Stay where it's predictable."*

And perhaps the greatest cost of all is this: the box steals your identity. Not by force, but by convincing you that survival is the same as living. But it's not. The truth is—you were never meant to live confined. You were not designed for boxes: you were designed for open spaces, for movement, for growth, for relationships that are safe, and futures that are hopeful.

Breaking out of the box is messy and slow. It requires courage. It requires safe people. It requires relearning what freedom feels like. But the cost of staying confined is always higher than the cost of breaking out. Because outside the box is where healing happens. Where identity can be rebuilt. Where trust can be restored. Where anger can soften and hope can rise again.

5 EDGES THAT PULLED ME IN

Let's examine the first way we find ourselves inside a box — by unknowingly walking into it. We can inadvertently walk into a box by not truly listening to and trusting the counsel of others, whether it's a parent, friend, or mentor. It could be by not following God—trusting Him—based on His Word and His Word alone. For some, we may hear from God, but instead of waiting on Him to move, we try to take matters into our own hands and then end up in a box, and then wonder how we ever got there. For some, it may mean not listening to the wisdom of others who have gone through a similar situation. For others, it may mean not observing and learning from the mistakes of other. These situations may sound like disobedience—our knowingly walking into a box—but are they?

We have to look at the intent of the heart to determine willful disobedience versus immaturity or the underdevelopment of the prefrontal cortex. The front part of the brain is responsible for executive functioning, and when it is not fully mature, it leads to difficulty with judgement, impulse control, planning and decision making. Studies from The National Library of Medicine suggest that a child's brain doesn't fully develop until the mid to late 20's. The maturation of the brain is influenced by hormones like estrogen, progesterone, and testosterone, but also heredity and environment. With that in mind, impulsive behavior and poor decision making is not always willful disobedience, but the inability to understand the consequences of decisions, even after being given clear warnings.

I have seven grandchildren, ranging in ages from 3 years to 17 years. If I tell my 5-year-old grandson not to cross the street because he could get it by a car, he does not understand the consequences like serious injury or death. He doesn't understand how that would affect his parents, siblings and extended family. Likewise, if I tell my oldest granddaughter not to have sex because it could result in pregnancy, a sexually transmitted disease, feelings of guilt and depression, separation from God—all of which can affect her future—future relationships, self-esteem, trust issues, etc., she wouldn't be able to see beyond the now.

Even adults, with a fully developed prefrontal cortex, sometimes can't look beyond the now, or what's right in front of them, and see how one choice can alter their future and affect the lives of others around them. A marital affair, for example, whether impulsive or planned, not only affects the individuals in the affair, it affects the other spouses, children, families, friendships, church communities, jobs and career opportunities, just to name a few.

A biblical example of unknowing walking into a box is witnessed in the story of Abraham and Sarah from the book of Genesis. God made a promise to Abraham that he would make his seed (offspring) as the dust of the earth. Some time went by and Sarah, Abraham's wife did not conceive a child. So, they decided to take matters into their own hands. Sarah gave Abraham her handmaiden, Hagar, to bear a child for Abraham. She conceived and bare Ishmael, but Ishmael was not the promised seed.

Let's stop here for just a moment. Was Abraham and Sarah disobedient? Yes, of course they were, but were they willfully disobeying God? I don't believe so. They heard what God said about them having a son, and they believed they would have one, but they thought God needed their help. Have you ever been in a situation where God has specifically told you something that was going to happen or given you a glimpse of the future, but instead of waiting on Him, you tried to speed up the process? It's not that we don't love God, but sometimes with our limited minds and our nature, we find it difficult to completely trust God and trust that He has it already worked out for us. Sometime we look at God the way we look at other people. We see their shortcomings and we see how humans make promises they don't keep, and it's hard to conceive of a God who is all knowing and all powerful and all loving.

We may have believed in promises a parent, an employer, a teacher or mentor has made, and those promises were not kept, so we find it difficult to believe that a God we cannot see will fulfill His promise. But unlike mankind, according to Numbers 23:19, "God is not a man, that He should lie."

Moving forward in the story, God told Abraham that Sarah would bear him a child in her old age, but Sarah doubted God. God reassured Abraham that he would visit Sarah at the appointed time and that she would have a son. Sarah conceived and bare Isaac. Now Abraham has two sons—from two different women. As the two boys got a little older, Ishmael, the son of the handmaiden—which we would now call the housekeeper—began to tease Isaac, making Sarah very upset. She told Abraham to send Hagar and Ishmael away. This was very distressing to Abraham. He was put in the middle because he loved both his sons, but God told him to listen to Sarah and send them away. So, he did.

If you would try to imagine the pain and anguish that Hagar, Ishmael, Sarah and Abraham felt. Abraham's actions had an effect—not only on himself—but also on others. His decisions caused hurt in the lives of other people because he did not completely trust that God would do what he said he was going to do.

> **"Trust in the Lord with all thine heart, and lean not unto thy own understanding. In all thy ways acknowledge him, and he shall direct thy paths." (Proverbs 3:5-6).**

Every aspect of our life should encompass God's will. No matter how small or insignificant it may seem to us; no matter how impossible it may appear to us, we must acknowledge God, and trust him and not lean on our own understanding. When we do, He will guide our steps in the right direction, avoiding boxes that lay waiting to encompass us.

We can also unknowingly walk into a box by not listening to and following God because we don't want to, or we think our way is better. It may be a situation that God has specifically told us to avoid, or to even run away from, but instead of listening, we do the opposite and walk right into the situation we were warned against. Sometimes it's a relationship, other times, a job or a business opportunity; other times it's refusing to do what we're asked to do or go where we've been directed to go. There are times as human beings that we believe we have enough will power or self-control to dip and dab in sin, and then think we will be able to walk away from it untouched or unaffected. But sin always comes with consequences.

I'll admit, sometimes we can walk away, and it seems that we have come out on the other side unscared—at least for the time being. But there are other times when we walk in and we are immediately stuck. And it may not necessarily be a sinful situation, but merely a place that is not God's best for us. Or it could be a situation in which God has given us an assignment, and instead of being obedient because of fear, we choose to run away from God's call.

But often enough, running away places us in circumstances where we find ourselves trapped in a box. And if we're fortunate enough to avoid getting stuck, we spend an enormous amount of time and energy getting out of a situation, and we end up right back where we started in the first place, and all we have for it is a lot of wasted time. Hopefully, we learn from those situations and think about how much further we would have gotten if we had only listened to God in the first place.

Let's look at the biblical story of Jonah. This story is a perfect example of someone who chose to run away from God's call. Jonah was instructed to go to the city of Nineveh to tell the people to repent because their wickedness was so great. But instead of obeying God, Jonah hid on a ship on its way to Tarshish because he didn't believe that the people of Nineveh deserved forgiveness. The Lord sent a mighty storm and the seamen discovered that Jonah was hiding on the ship.

After casting lots, they discovered that Jonah was responsible for the great tempest in the sea. Jonah told them to throw him overboard, so they did and the sea stopped raging. A great fish swallowed up Jonah, and he was in the belly of the fish three days and three nights.

Then Jonah prayed to God from the fish's belly and the Lord heard his prayer and spoke to the fish, and it vomited out Jonah upon the dry land. And the Lord spoke to Jonah again and told him to go to Nineveh, and this time he was obedient. Although the belly of the whale was a place of discomfort, it was also a place of protection.

Because of Jonah's disobedience, he caused a great storm on a ship and brought great fear to the seamen who were on the ship. Again, we see how one person's disobedience can affect the lives of others around or associated with him. Also, Jonah had to spend three days and nights inside the belly of a fish, which I'm certain caused him a tremendous amount of fear and anxiety. And after all that, he still ended up back where he started and doing what God wanted him to do from the beginning.

"I will instruct thee and teach thee in the way which thou shalt go: I will guide thee with my eye" (Psalm 32:8). Can you imagine God guiding us with His eye? He sees all and knows all. He knows where we've been, where we're going, where we should go, and what will happen if we go. He sees the future, he has seen the future, been to the end and back and it is his will to instruct us and teach us which way to go. If we only trust Him, listen, and obey.

Now I want to speak to the skeptics. I recall a conversation with an old friend of mine several years ago. This friend asked me, "You can't really believe that a whale swallowed a man and he survived in its belly?" I responded, "Yes, I do." This friend went on to say, "You know that's just a fable and the belly represents a place of safety or a state of mind where you realize the error of your ways." Whether you believe it literally or figuratively, there is still a lesson to be learned.

My response now is that I choose to believe it literally. But most importantly, even if you don't, what we can all learn from this story is that many times we are given second chances. Sometimes we walk into situations that we know we shouldn't walk into, walk away from projects, dreams, business ideas or directives we're given, and are given second chances. Sometimes those dreams come back to life. Sometimes someone least expected walks into our life and changes the trajectory of our path. Sometimes we have to experience pain, fear or anxiety before we are able to fulfill the mission and vision laid out for us. But there are also times when second chances don't come our way. Sometimes decisions lead to destruction; sometimes disappointment, and for some death.

Whether you believe the story of Jonah is merely a fable, or if you believe it to be a true-life experience, the lesson remains the same. When we unknowingly walk into a box, look for that second chance opportunity when one presents itself. For Jonah, his life was spared; he was given a second chance to choose differently.

6 DRIFTING INTO THE DIM

The second way we get ourselves into boxes is by being drawn into one. I believe that the enemy is on a mission. And his mission is to find out what our weaknesses are, and then to attack us in those areas. He studies to see what is appealing to us, what attracts us or gets our attention, as well as, what bothers us or frustrates us and causes us to feel that we have to do something out of fear. For me, the enemy is a thief that comes to steal, kill and destroy, as stated in the book of John.

We see an example of someone being drawn in from the book of Genesis. Isaac had twins: two sons, Esau and Jacob. Isaac loved Esau because he was a was a hunter and he ate venison, but Rebekah, Isaac's wife, loved Jacob. One day Esau came in from the field and was very faint, and Jacob was cooking some stew. Esau asked Jacob for some stew. Jacob told Esau that if he sold him, that day, his birthright, he would give him some stew. Esau told him that he was to the point of death so what good would a birthright do to him. Jacob made Esau promise that he would sell it to him, then Jacob gave Esau some bread and stew. Esau gave up all the rights and benefits of being the firstborn for a little food. The little food became the instrument of separation. The little food became the enemy.

Esau was hungry, but fulfilling that instant gratification caused him to lose his inheritance. Inheritance meant so much more in the Bible days than it does now. Being the first born meant receiving all the blessings and responsibilities of being the head of the family. This included certain privileges, including material wealth and decision-making power. Our birthright as Christians is to inherit all that God is in Christ. All the authority and power that Christ had on the earth has been passed on to us. "But if the Spirit of him that raised up Jesus from the dead dwell in you, he that raised up Christ from the dead shall also quicken your mortal bodies by his Spirit that dwelleth in you" (Romans 8:11). I had heard and read that scripture, but when I first understood it with revelation knowledge, it took my faith to a new level.

In Esau's case, his enemy was his hunger and the need to fulfill that desire. What is your enemy? The enemy can be many things. Is it those seductive lyrics in a song that you can't get out of your mind, the pornography on television or on social media, like Tik Tok, Instagram and Facebook? Is it the beautiful woman who smiles at you at work after a disagreement with your wife, the young man that tells you how he would treat you if he were your man? Could it be the friend who slept with your boyfriend, the relative that owes you money, the co-worker who got the promotion over you, the man who molested you, the church member who judged you, the wine sitting on the shelf, the lure of easy money on the streets, the casino…...? The list goes on. Looking at Esau, the meal he consumed was instant gratification. Did he consider that giving into his flesh would affect the rest of his life; did he fathom that his one decision would alter his destiny forever.

"Be sober, be vigilant; because your adversary the devil, as a roaring lion, walketh about, seeking whom he may devour" (I Peter 5:8). The enemy's mission is to attack us in those weak areas and then devour us. He makes things look so appealing and attractive that we are drawn in. The dull appears shiny; the grass always looks greener on the other side. We don't realize until we cross that line, that it was a box—drawing us in and leaving us trapped—left alone to bear the aftermath. Whether it's a job with an enormous salary, or an intimate relationship that you think is love, but later discover that it was only lust, or whether it's a financial investment that eventually has you bound by debt; the initial attraction drew you in. And Satan knows what is attractive to us and what will draw us away from God, so we must constantly be aware of our adversary.

7 THE LURE OF THE LESSOR SPACE

The third way we find ourselves in boxes is by being tricked in. The perfect example of someone being tricked is Eve in the book of Genesis. After God created Adam and Eve, he placed them in the garden of Eden. Adam and Eve were without sin, and had a perfect relationship with God. God told them they could eat from every tree in the garden except from the tree of the knowledge of good and evil. Why is it that we want the one thing we're not supposed to have?

> **Now the serpent was more subtil than any beast of the field which the LORD God had made. And he said unto the woman, Yea, hath God said, Ye shall not eat of every tree of the garden? And the woman said unto the serpent, We may eat of the fruit of the trees of the garden: But of the fruit of the tree which is in the midst of the garden, God hath said, Ye shall not eat of it, neither shall ye touch it, lest ye die. And the serpent said unto the woman, Ye shall not surely die: For God doth know that in the day ye eat thereof, then your eyes shall be opened, and ye shall be as**

> gods, knowing good and evil. And when the woman saw that the tree was good for food, and that it was pleasant to the eyes, and a tree to be desired to make one wise, she took of the fruit thereof, and did eat, and gave also unto her husband with her; and he did eat. (Genesis 3:1-6).

Because of their disobedience, they were punished and sent out of the Garden — separated from the presence of God. In that moment, humanity unknowingly walked into the first box — a box built from deception, desire, and disobedience. What looked beautiful and harmless became the very thing that enclosed them, cutting them off from intimacy with their Creator.

Just like Eve, we too can find ourselves walking into boxes without realizing it. The enemy rarely shows us the whole picture; he entices us with what looks good, feels right, or promises wisdom, success, or love. What begins as curiosity or desire can quietly become captivity. Being tricked is slightly different from being drawn in. When we are drawn into something, we willingly go in, but we are given a little push or a nudge and we may not be completely sure about it. But being tricked is when we are completed deceived. We honestly believe that what we are doing is the right thing and it's not until we are completed engulfed in something that the truth is then revealed to us. Deception always paints itself pretty, never revealing the darkness beneath.

> Beware of false prophets, which come to you in sheep's clothing, but inwardly they are ravening wolves. Ye shall know them by their fruits. Do men gather grapes of thorns, or figs of thistles? (Matthew 7:15-16).

We might walk into a box through compromise — choosing what feels convenient over what is right. We might step into one through fear — staying silent when we should speak, or holding back when we should move forward. Sometimes we enter boxes through pain — trying to protect ourselves from hurt, only to end up isolated and disconnected. Other times, we simply believe the lies whispered to our hearts: *You're not enough. You'll never change. God has forgotten you.*

By the time we realize where we are, the door has already closed behind us. Yet even then, all is not lost. The same Spirit that raised Jesus from the dead still lives within us. That power has never left — it's the key that unlocks every box we've ever walked into.

We have to be able to discern when we are hearing from God and when we are being deceived. The enemy is cunning, and his lies often sound close to the truth. The only way to recognize the difference is by knowing God's voice — and that comes through spending time with Him. When we walk closely with God, His voice becomes familiar. It carries peace, conviction, and clarity — never confusion, fear, or shame. But when we neglect time in His presence, the noise of the world grows louder, and deception becomes easier to believe. Intimacy with God sharpens our discernment. It's in prayer, worship, and studying His Word that we learn to distinguish truth from imitation, guidance from distraction, and freedom from the subtle boxes meant to bind us.

8 WHEN THE WALLS START WHISPERING

The fourth way we find ourselves in a box is deliberately walk into one. Before we look at deliberately walking into the box, let's look again at intent of the heart. In the first story of Esau, he forsakes his inheritance to meet an immediate need. The other story of Esau in Genesis is an example of willfully walking into a box when he married the daughter of Ishmael. Remember that Ishmael was the son of Abraham, conceived by Sarah's handmaiden Hagar. Even though Ishmael was not the promised son of Abraham, the bible tells us that God specifically states that he would make Ishmael a great nation because he was Abraham's son.

We know in Genesis that Isaac had instructed his son Jacob to marry one of the daughters of Laban, and not a Canaanite woman, because they worshipped idols and engaged in practices that were offensive to God. Esau married his first two wives from the daughters of Heth, against his parent's wishes.

When Esau heard that Abraham had told Jacob not to marry a Canaanite woman, out of wounded pride, Easu deliberately went and married Mahalath, the daughter of Ishmael. Instead of seeking God's direction, he made another decision driven by emotion—marrying into Ishmael's family, thinking it would somehow restore his standing. But his choice was not rooted in obedience; it was rooted in reaction. We know that Esau had already sold his birthright for a meal, which mean forsaking his right to be buried in the Cave of the Patriarchs. Why is this important?

Patriarchs: Abraham, Isaac, Jacob, Sarah, Rebecca, and Leah. According to Jewish mystical tradition, it's also the entrance to the Garden of Eden where Adam and Eve are buried. According to the Midrash, the Patriarchs are said not to be dead but "sleeping". They rise to beg mercy for their children throughout the generations. After Jacob's death, he was taken to be buried in the cave of Machpelah and Esau disrupted the

The cave of Machpelah, in the West Bank city of Hebron, is the burial place of the Matriarchs and funeral processional, claiming he had the right to be buried in the cave. However, after Naphtali, the sixth son of Jacob received the document stating that Esau had sold his birthright, which gave Jacob rights to the cave, Chushim, Jacob's deaf grandson, severed Esau's head. According to Got Questions Ministries, It is believed that his head remains in the lap of Isaac to this day.

Again, Eau's impulsive actions shows us an illustration of willfully stepping into a box of his own making—a box built from pride, hurt, and the desire for approval. Many of us have done the same. When we feel rejected, overlooked, or misunderstood, we sometimes make choices to prove a point rather than to pursue God's purpose. We enter relationships, careers, or situations that look right in the moment but lead us further from the peace and promise God intended. Esau's story reminds us that not every open door is from God. Sometimes, what appears to be an opportunity is actually a box — one that limits our growth, blinds our judgment, and separates us from His best.

9 BOUND BY ACCIDENT

The fifth way we find ourselves in a box is jumping in and hoping to jump back out. Let's look Peter's denial of Jesus that is found in all four Gospels. On the night Jesus was arrested, He told His disciple Peter that before the rooster crowed the next morning, Peter would deny knowing Him three times. Peter insisted that he would never do such a thing and that he would even die for Jesus if necessary. Later that night, after Jesus was taken away to be questioned by the high priest, Peter followed at a distance and waited in the courtyard. While he was there, several people recognized him as one of Jesus' followers. Each time they accused him, Peter denied it—first to a servant girl, then to another bystander, and finally to a group who insisted they had seen him with Jesus. Immediately after Peter's third denial, the rooster crowed, just as Jesus had said. Realizing what he had done, Peter was overcome with sorrow and wept bitterly.

Did Peter deny Jesus? Absolutely. Do you believe he intended to deny Him or planned to deny Him? I would have to say, No. Why did Peter deny Him? I think sometimes we find ourselves in a box; we never planned to walk into a box. In fact, we may even think to ourselves, *"Okay, I'm gonna jump in this box, but jump right back out when it's safe."* So why did he deny Jesus. I would guess that most of us would say fear. But what kind of fear? Was Peter afraid for his own life? I'm not so sure. If his fear was not of death, then what was it?

I would argue that Peter's fear was ridicule or being teased or treated with contempt. We know that Jesus had already told the disciples during the last supper that someone would be offended and that Peter would deny him three times before the rooster would crow the next morning. "And as they were eating, Jesus took bread, and blessed it, and brake it, and gave it to the disciples, and said, Take, eat; this is my body." Then saith Jesus unto them, "All ye shall be offended because of me this night" (Matthew 26:31). In this passage, the word offended means to *stumble* or be caused to fall. In the original Greek, the word used for offended is *skandalon*, which refers to a trap or a stumbling block. It doesn't just mean they would be angry, but that they would be so shocked and dismayed that their faith would falter.

Remember, Peter was the same man who cut the ear off of the high priest's servant. On the night Jesus was betrayed, He went with His disciples to the Garden of Gethsemane to pray. As He finished praying, a crowd approached, led by Judas Iscariot—one of His own disciples—who had agreed to betray Him to the religious leaders. The crowd carried swords and clubs, sent by the chief priests and elders to arrest Jesus. When the soldiers moved to seize Him, Peter—in a burst of fear and misguided courage—drew his sword and struck the servant of the high priest, cutting off his right ear. The servant's name was Malchus. But Jesus immediately intervened.

And Jesus said unto him, Friend, wherefore art thou come? Then came they, and laid hands on Jesus and took him. And, behold, one of them which were with Jesus stretched out his hand, and drew his sword, and struck a servant of the high priest's, and smote off his ear. Then said Jesus unto him, Put up again thy sword into his place: for all they that take the sword shall perish with the sword. (Matthew 26: 50-52).

After seeing this, Jesus reached out and touched the servant's ear and healed him. Jesus reminded Peter that He wanted to, He could call on His Father for more than twelve legions of angels. In other words, He reminded Peter that He didn't need him to stand up for him or protect him.

We can conclude that Peter was not afraid of death the day he denied being a follower of Jesus. Peter was in fact the apostle who promised to be faithful to Jesus, even unto death. If it wasn't fear of death, was it shame or fear of being ostracized? Today, many believers attend church every Sunday but look around at a restaurant to see who's watching before they bow their heads to say grace, or hesitate to say the name of Jesus at work or in the grocery store. Many Christians read their bibles every day, but hesitate to pray with a co-worker who is experiencing a traumatic event. Many believers of Christ will speak openly about their faith when surrounded by other believers, but will remain quiet in the presence of unbelievers.

The account of Peter's denial of Jesus is found in all four of the Gospels, but I would like for us to read John's account in John 18. In John's account, we learn that the temple police had arrested Jesus, tied

Him, and led him away to appear before Annas, father-in-law to Caiaphas, the current high priest. John reveals that Peter was not the only one who followed Jesus back to from Gethsemane to the home of Annas.

Jesus had been betrayed by Judas and arrested by the temple police in the Garden of Gethsemane. While this was happening, Simon Peter was following Jesus, as was another disciple. That disciple was an acquaintance of the high priest; he went with Jesus into the high priest's courtyard. But Peter remained standing outside by the door. The other disciple, the one known to the high priest, went out and spoke to the girl who was the doorkeeper and brought Peter in. Peter denied knowing Jesus when asked by a slave girl. Was Peter afraid of a little slave girl? What could she have possibly done to him? The book of John provides another historical note.

> **Now the slaves and the temple police had made a charcoal fire, because it was cold. They were standing there warming themselves, and Peter was standing with them, warming himself. (John 18:18).**

Annas, the former high priest, who was still a major influence among the religious leaders in Jerusalem questioned Jesus. Why is this significant? Annas was significant in the Bible as a powerful, influential figure who, even after being removed as high priest, continued to wield immense power through his family and his role in the trial of Jesus.

Let's look a little deeper into Peter's character and the story how he walked on the water in Matthew. After feeding the five thousand, Jesus told His disciples to get into the boat and go ahead of Him to the other side of the Sea of Galilee while He went up on a mountain to pray alone. As night fell, the disciples' boat was far out on the water, being battered by strong winds and heavy waves. The storm made it difficult for them to row, and fear began to rise among them. Then, sometime between three and six in the morning, they saw something—someone—walking toward them on the water! Terrified, they cried out, "It's a ghost!" (Matthew 14:26, NKJV). And immediately Jesus tried to comfort them by telling them not to be afraid. Peter, still unsure asked if he could walk out to the water. Jesus responded and directed him to come. Peter stepped out of the boat. With his eyes fixed on Jesus, he began walking on the water—doing what no one else had ever done! But then he noticed the strong wind and crashing waves around him. Fear crept in, and as his focus shifted away from Jesus, he began to sink. Desperate, Peter cried out for the Lord to save him.

> **"And immediately Jesus stretched forth His hand and caught him and said unto him, 'O thou of little faith, why didst thou doubt?' And when they had come into the boat, the wind ceased. Then those who were in the boat came and worshipped Him, saying, 'In truth Thou art the Son of God'" (Matthew 14:31-33).**

There Is evidence in the New Testament that Peter had a problem with the fear of ridicule. Before going to the home of Cornelius in Acts chapter ten, Peter He took some Jewish friends with him. It is believed that he wanted to have Jewish witnesses with him who could testify as to his involvement with the Gentiles. Peter became a backslider in

Antioch. At the Jerusalem Conference, it was agreed that Gentiles are saved the same way as Jews, by grace.

Paul tells us that Peter joined in the fellowship with Gentiles, until he looked up and saw some Jews from Jerusalem there, and he withdrew himself from the Gentiles in a manner that jeopardized the victory. "But when I saw that they were deviating from the truth of the gospel, I told Cephas in front of everyone, 'If you, who are a Jew, live like a Gentile and not like a Jew, how can you compel Gentiles to live like Jews?" (Gal 2:11-14). Paul referred to Peter's actions as hypocrisy.

In Acts 2, Peter didn't show any signs of this fear on the day of Pentecost, when he preached the first sermon following the Ascension of our Lord—not fear of physical retaliation. Peter denied Christ and jumped into his box. His box was the fear of ridicule. Like Peter, sometimes we jump into a box—whether planned or unplanned—with the intent that we'll jump back out as soon as we can. Sometimes we jump into boxes, never intending to stay bound. Peter repented after denying His Lord; He confessed his sin and became a mighty witness for Christ, but I can only imagine the shame he must have felt when he jumped into his box—knowing he had denied the One he had followed. He denied being a follower of Christ.

His life after that betrayal teaches us that the Lord forgave him and gave him the victory. **We can also be forgiven because God shows no favouritism. His mercy isn't reserved for a select few, nor is His grace limited** to those who seem most worthy.

> **Then Peter opened his mouth and said, "Of a truth I perceive that God is no respecter of persons: but in every**

nation he that feareth him, and worketh righteousness, is accepted with him." (Acts 10:34-35).

We may be able to bounce back out of a box and sometimes we may learn a valuable lesson through that experience, but we must also acknowledge that it may also come with a price—separation from God. Like Peter, jumping in a box doesn't have to be the end. I believe that Peter's experience empowered him to be a powerful witness for Christ, as we see in the first chapters of Acts.

Peter was not perfect, as we are not perfect. One of the greatest lessons we learn from the story of Peter is how to deal with past sin. One thing the enemy tries to do is convince us that we cannot be forgiven; he tries to convince us that God will not forgive us and that we are not worthy of forgiveness. But as we see in this story, Peter went on to help establish the church and he also wrote many books in the bible. God is not looking for perfection. He is willing to forgive; He wants to forgive. All we have to do is repent.

10 THE CAPTURE

The sixth way we find ourselves in a box is being pushed into the box. The example I am using to illustrate this is the biblical story of Joseph in the book of Genesis, when his brothers threw him into a pit in Genesis 37. This familiar story is a biblical account of jealousy and how jealousy leads to sinful acts. Like all sinful acts, sin leads to consequences. Sometimes we end up in a box, not of our own will, but because we are thrown into one because of jealousy and resentment.

Jacob, also called Israel, lived in the land of Canaan—the same land where his father had once been a stranger. Joseph, his beloved son, was only seventeen years old when he was tending the flocks with his brothers, the sons of Bilhah and Zilpah, his father's wives. Joseph often brought his father reports about their behavior, which stirred resentment among his brothers. He wasn't trying to gossip; the text suggests he was honest, responsible, and deeply loyal to Jacob. However, for his brothers his behavior was seen as betrayal.

Now Israel loved Joseph more than all his children, because he was the son of his old age: and he made him a

coat of many colours. And when his brethren saw that their father loved him more than all his brethren, they hated him, and could not speak peaceably unto him" (Genesis 37:1–4).

Joseph's story begins with favor but quickly turns into rejection. The same brothers who should have celebrated him, became the ones who plotted against him—proof that sometimes the people closest to us can become the very source of our deepest pain.

As the story continues, Joseph dreamed a dream and told it to his brothers. He shared that in his dream, he and his brothers were binding sheaves in the field, and his sheaf—a bundle of cut grain stalks tied together—arose and stood upright; and his brother's sheaves surrounded it and bowed down to his sheaf. After he finished telling them the story, they asked him if he would rule over them. And they hated him even more because of his dreams, and for his words.

If we examine the passage, Joseph had done nothing wrong. He had a dream and shared it with his brothers. Because in his dream, he had dominion over his brothers, they hated him for it. Sometimes people will hate you simply because of a dream. Whether it's a literal dream or a dream or vision for your life, often times, you may be hated because of your dreams. I've heard many wise people say to be careful who you share your dreams with because not everyone wants the best for you. Sometimes when people lack dreams of their own, jealousy kicks in and turns to hate because you do have a dreams and aspirations.

Later on, Joseph's brothers were out working in the fields feeding their father's flock. Joseph's father sent him to find his brothers. A man found Joseph wandering in the field and asked him where he was going.

Joseph told the man that he was looking for his brothers who had left home to feed their flocks. The man told Joseph that they had been there, but had left and were headed to Dothan. Joseph continued on his journey and ended up finding them in Dothan. When they saw Joseph approaching from a distance, they conspired against him to kill him. They spoke amongst themselves, referring to him as the *dreamer*. They plotted to kill him and throw him in a pit and tell everyone that an evil beast had killed him. But Rueben, the oldest brother, pleaded with his brothers not to kill Joseph, but to throw him into a well in the wilderness in hopes that he would be able to take him back to their father.

When Joseph approached them, they tore his coat of many colors off of him that was a gift from his father and threw him into the empty well. A short while later, they saw a group of Ishmaelites coming from Gilead on their way to Egypt. Judah then asked his brothers why should they kill Joseph and hide it when they could sell him to the Ishmaelites. When a Midianite merchants passed by, they pulled Joseph out of the well and sold him for twenty pieces of silver. When I think about this story, even when it looks like everyone is against you, God has a greater plan and will use someone to fight for you. If there had been no Reuben, Joseph's brothers likely would have taken his life. But God made sure there was a *Reuben*—someone who fought for him, even when he couldn't fight for himself. I'm sure we all have someone looking out for us, praying for us, advocating for us, most time without our knowledge. God often sends a *Reuben*—someone who steps in, maybe quietly, but powerfully, to protect, to comfort, or to show love when it's needed most.

When Reuben returned to the pit; he saw that Joseph was not there and he was so upset that he tore his clothes off because he didn't know how he was going to explain it to their father. So, the brothers killed a kid of the goats and dipped Joseph's coat of many colors in the blood. They took the coat back to their father and pretended not to know it was Joseph's coat. When Jacob saw the coat, he knew it was the coat he had given Joseph and believed that a wild animal must have killed Joseph and devoured him to pieces.

The Midianites sold him into Egypt to Potiphar, an officer of Pharaoh, who was a captain of the guard. The LORD was with Joseph, and he was a prosperous man; and he was in the house of his master, the Egyptian. When his master saw that the LORD was with Joseph, he was gracious to him and made him overseer over his house, and all that he had, he put into his hand. The Lord blessed the Egyptian's house because of Joseph. The Egyptian's wife thought Joseph was very handsome and she asked him to have sex with her. Joseph refused, explaining to her that God had blessed him and he couldn't sin against God.

As the story goes on, she continued to ask him to sleep with her and each time he refused, she became very angry. The last time she approached him, he tried to leave the house and she grabbed his garment and told the men of her house that he tried to rape her. When her husband got home, the men told him what his wife had said and Joseph's master took him, and put him into the prison, a place where the king's prisoners were held. Joseph would have surely been put to death if the Lord had not been on his side. This an example of God's covering. As we go through life, we are sure to face situations where we are lied on, falsely accused, blamed for something we had nothing to do with. But God! He is a God of Truth. He is Truth! And no weapon formed against us will prosper.

But the LORD was with Joseph, and shewed him mercy, and gave him favor in the sight of the keeper of the prison and put him in charge of the other prisoners. While in prison, Joseph interprets the dreams of two prisoners, the king's cupbearer and his baker. Joseph asked the cupbearer to remember him when he is released from prison. However, when he gets released, he forgets that Joseph had asked him to remember him and to tell Pharaoh how he had interpreted his dream. Even in prison, even in an unfavorable situation, the Lord is always a present help in time of trouble, and will never leave us for forsake us.

One day, Pharaoh had a dream that no one could interpret for him. His chief cupbearer then remembered that Joseph had interpreted a dream for him when he was in prison two years earlier. After two years, Pharaoh dreamed that he was standing by the Nile, and coming up out of the Nile were seven plump, beautiful and healthy cows that fed in the reed grass. Seven other, ugly and thin, came up out of the Nile after them, and stood by the other cows on the bank of the Nile. The ugly thin cows ate up the seven attractive, plump cows. When Pharaoh woke up, he fell asleep again and dreamed a second time. In the next dream, seven ears of grain, plump and good, were growing on one stalk. After that, sprouted seven ears, thin and blighted by the east wind. The thin ears swallowed up the seven plump, full ears. After Pharaoh woke up, he realized it was a dream. In the morning, he was troubled, and he sent and called for all the magicians of Egypt and all its wise men. Pharaoh told them his dreams, but no one was able to interpret his dreams.

Then the chief cupbearer told Pharaoh that he remembered when he was in prison a young Hebrew had interpreted his dream and the dream of the baker. He went on to tell him that both interpretations came to pass as he was restored to his office and the baker was hanged, exactly as Joseph had said. Then Pharaoh sent and called Joseph, and they quickly brought him out of prison. After Joseph had shaved and changed his clothes, he came in before Pharaoh. He told Joseph that he had a dream that no one was able to interpret, and he had heard from the cupbearer that he could interpret dreams. Joseph made sure to tell Pharaoh that he didn't interpret the dream, but that God had given him the interpretation.

Pharaoh went on to share the dream. Joseph told Pharaoh that his two dreams were one dream. He told him that the seven good cows are seven years, and the seven good ears are seven years. The seven lean and ugly cows that came up after them are seven years, and the seven empty ears blighted by the east wind are also seven years of famine. God had shown to Pharaoh what he was about to do. There will come seven years of great plenty throughout all the land of Egypt, but after them, there will arise seven years of famine, and all the plenty will be forgotten in the land of Egypt. The famine will consume the land, and the plenty will be unknown in the land by reason of the famine that will follow, for it will be very severe. Joseph told him that because he dreamed two dreams with the same meaning, that meant that it was fixed by God and that God will bring it to pass very soon.

Joseph proposed to Pharaoh that he should appoint overseers over the land and told them to take one-fifth of the produce of the land of Egypt during the seven plentiful years, and let them gather all the food of these good years that are coming and store up grain under the authority of Pharaoh for food in the cities, and let them keep it. That food shall be a reserve for the land against the seven years of famine that are to occur in the land of Egypt, so that the land may not perish through the famine. (Genesis 41)

This proposal pleased Pharaoh and all his servants. And Pharaoh said to his servants, "Can we find such a one as this is, a man in whom the Spirit of God is" (Genesis 41:38). Then Pharaoh told Joseph that because God had shown him this, he declared that there was no one as discerning and wise as he was. He appointed him over his house, and that the people in his house will do everything he commands them to do. He also declared that in regard to the throne that only Pharaoh would be greater than he was. Then Pharaoh told Joseph to look out over the land of Egypt and see everything he had given him authority over. Pharaoh took his signet ring from his hand and put it on Joseph's hand, and clothed him in garments of fine linen and put a gold chain about his neck. And he made him ride in his second chariot.

> **Pharaoh makes Joseph ride in his second chariot and has people proclaim his authority, stating, "And Pharaoh said unto Joseph, See, I have set thee over all the land of Egypt". He also gives Joseph his authority, saying, "I am Pharaoh, and without thee shall no man lift up his hand or foot in all the land of Egypt. (Genesis 41:43-44)**

And Pharaoh changed Joseph's name to Zaphenath-paneah and gave him in marriage to Asenath, the daughter of Potiphera priest of On. So, Joseph went out over the land of Egypt. Joseph was thirty years old when Pharaoh, the king of Egypt appointed him overseer. During the next seven years when the earth produced abundantly, all the food was gathered from the fields around the cities and stored. It is said it was so much grain like the sand of the sea. It was so much that it couldn't be measured. After the seven years of abundance, seven years of famine began to come, as Joseph had interpreted from the dream. The famine had spread over all the land and Joseph began to sell to the Egyptians and when the word spread, all the earth came to Egypt to bury grain.

Jacob, Joseph's father heard that there was corn in Egypt and told him sons to travel to Egypt to buy grain. Jacob wouldn't let Benjamin, his youngest son, go because he was afraid something bad might happen to him. He loved Benjamin because he was Joseph's only full brother, sons of his wife Rachel, whom he loved. When the brothers got to Egypt, Joseph recognized them, but they did not know he was their brother. Joseph asked them if they were spies and they tried to convince them that they weren't and had come to buy food. They explained that they are twelve brothers, the son of one man, but the youngest didn't come with them. Joseph put them in jail for 3 days because he remembered what they had done to him. After 3 days, he told them that if they were honest men and not really spies, for them to prove it by going to get their little brother. Joseph told them that one brother had to stay in prison and the rest of them could carry corn home and bring their youngest brother back with them. The brothers began arguing amongst themselves and blaming each other for their hardship because they had sold Joseph to the Ishmaelites.

Joseph heard them and understood them because he had an interpreter with him and he walked away from them crying. When he returned, he ordered Simeon to be bound and thrown back in prison. He then commanded to fill their sacks with corn, and to put their money they had paid for the corn back in their sacks. On the way back home, one of them opened his sack and saw that the money was back in his sack and they were afraid, wondering what God had done to them. When they arrived home, they told their father Jacob everything that had happened. He was so bereaved he thought Joseph was dead, Simeon had been left in Egypt as collateral and they wanted to take Benjamin away. He didn't want Benjamin to go because he was afraid, he would lose him too, but Judah convinced his father that he would take him back to Egypt and if he didn't return, he would take personal responsibility for Benjamin.

Jacob sent them away with gifts and double the amount of silver that was put back in their sacks. As the story continues, the brothers arrived back in Egypt with Benjamin, Joseph prepares a great feast for them and Benjamin's portion was five times that of his brothers. Joseph instructed his steward to fill their sacks with food and silver and to put his personal silver cup in Benjamin's sack.

After they left and were on their journey back home, Joseph orders his steward to catch up with them, and of course Joseph's silver cup was found in Benjamin's sack. Joseph announced that Benjamin would have to stay and be his slave since the cup was found in his cup. Judah pleaded with Joseph and told him that he couldn't return home without Benjamin because he had promised his father that Benjamin would be safe. Finally, Joseph reveals himself to his brothers and naturally they were terrified. He told them that although they threw him in a pit, sold him and he ended up in Egypt, it was not them who sent him there, but it was God. God had made him Lord over all of Egypt. (Genesis 44,45)

What I love about this story is that what man means for evil, God uses for good. Joseph was indeed pushed in a box. What looked like death to Joseph ended up life. Not only was Joseph elevated to a position of leadership in Egypt, he was also used as an instrument to bless the very ones who meant him hard. What's important to remember is that when your ways please the Lord, even when it looks like there's no way out, God has a plan, and God knows our future, and we have to trust that He is in control. Although Joseph was angry and hurt by what his brothers had done to him, he didn't let his anger dictate his choice to do good.

11 THE UNNOTICED DESCENT

The seventh way to get in a box is Unknowingly placed in a box. Moses was unknowingly place in a box at birth. By the end of the Genesis, the Israelites had achieved well respected immigrant status in the land of Egypt. The Egyptians had welcomed the Hebrew foreigners from Canaan because they were family to Joseph who, even as a non-Egyptian, had risen to second-in-command next to Pharaoh. There came a disruption when a new king arose over Egypt, who unfortunately did not know Joseph (Exodus 1:8). Israel's status declined rapidly from welcomed guests to feared foreigners and oppressed slaves.

> **And the fame thereof was heard in Pharaoh's house, saying, Joseph's brethren are come: and it pleased Pharaoh well, and his servants. And Pharaoh said unto Joseph, "Say unto thy brethren, This do ye; lade your beasts, and go, get you unto the land of Canaan; And take**

> your father and your households, and come unto me: and I will give you the good of the land of Egypt, and ye shall eat the fat of the land. Now thou art commanded, this do ye; take you wagons out of the land of Egypt for your little ones, and for your wives, and bring your father, and come. Also regard not your stuff; for the good of all the land of Egypt is your's. (Genesis 45:16-20)

From a 2008 commentary by Dennis Olson, the text highlights how politics, ethnic identity, and religion together create a volatile environment that can lead to either great good or great evil. A political strategy for new leaders, whether an Egyptian pharaoh or a Nazi Hitler, involves trying to gain power by singling out a perceived weaker minority or outsider group and calling them the enemy. We see this all through history. Fear of others is a powerful source of unity. What people don't understand, or what people fear, they naturally try to eliminate, control and/or attempt to make inferior.

If we look at the book of Exodus, the Hebrew population is growing in Egypt and what was once a minority begins to be a threat against the existing power. Olson (2008) explains that while Genesis presents the growing Israelite population as a sign of God's faithfulness, Pharaoh views the same growth as a frightening danger to Egypt's safety and culture. Although the Israelites were not a threat to the Egyptians if we look at it in the natural. However, God was with them and Pharaoh feared that their growing numbers and possibility that they may join with other nations against Egypt was indeed a threat. What does a government do when their power is threatened? Pharaoh responds by trying three different, but ultimately unsuccessful strategies, to stem the growth of the Israelite people: Pharaoh enslaves the Israelites, commands midwives to kill Hebrew boys at birth, and commands all Egyptians to throw Hebrew boys into the Nile River. (Exodus 1)

In the first chapter of the book of Exodus, Pharaoh forces the Israelites into slavery. The Bible confirms that the Israelites were to build two supply cities, Pithom and Ramses, not far from Goshen, the city where Jacob and his descendants were disbursed. The cities served as the main places for the distribution of goods. The Pharaoh controlled these cities, ultimately giving him power and control. Does this sound familiar? All through history, a select group controls the majority of goods and services from the top, ultimately leading to oppression and economic stability for the majority. One thing to point out is that Israelites were God's chosen people, and throughout Pharaoh's tactics, they are victorious and reminded that with God there is protection, provision, deliverance and promotion.

Now, let's look closely at the biblical account of the story of Moses. In the first chapter of the book of Exodus, a new king comes into power who doesn't know anything about Joseph. He sees that the Israelite people are growing in numbers and fears that they will join with their enemies and overtake them. He tells the Hebrew midwives that when they are helping with the delivery during childbirth, that they should kill the baby if it's a boy, but if it's a girl to let her live.

Like any system of oppression, the majority has been very strategic in eliminating what they fear to be a threat. Pharaoh wanted to eliminate the boys because he knew they could grow up and resist their oppressor. Similarly, to today, young boys and men of color are strategically eliminated by infiltrating drugs and guns within communities, imposing obstacles to furthering education, unfair hiring practices and wrongful imprisonment.

As the story unfolds, the midwives refused because they feared God. When confronted by the king, they claimed that the deliveries happened so fast before they would arrive and they were not able to kill the baby boys as ordered. The bible tells us that because the midwives feared God, He gave them families of their own. Sometimes we have to stand up for what's right, even when it goes against what someone in authority over us tells us to do.

Moses' mother defies the order to kill her son and conceals him until he becomes too old to hide. She then places him in a basket on the Nile. Many scholars say this was a deliberate attempt to have Moses adopted because his older sister was watching nearby. The basket, containing the three-month-old baby Moses, was placed in reeds by the river bank (presumably the Nile) to protect him from the Egyptian mandate to drown every male Hebrew child.

As we know, the baby was found by Pharaoh's daughter. Later on, Pharaoh's daughter came down to bathe in the river while her young attendants walked along the bank nearby. Pharaoh's daughter noticed the basket and instructed her maid to bring it to her. Moses' sister is watching this whole time. She comes out of hiding and asked Pharaoh's daughter if she would like her to find a Hebrew woman to nurse the child for her. So, she went and fetched the infant's mother. Pharaoh's daughter even offered to pay her to nurse the child. She was paid to nurse and care for her own son.

No matter what family you're born into, who your parents are, what president is in leadership, what laws are implemented, when you are chosen by God for a specific purpose, as quoted in Isaiah 54:17 "No weapon formed against you shall prosper." We know that Moses was adopted by Pharaoh's daughter and lived in the house of Pharaoh. The bible tells us that when Moses had grown up, he went out to observe his people, who were the Hebrews, and he saw their oppression and also witnessed an Egyptian beating one of his Hebrew brothers. Moses didn't see anyone looking so he beat the Egyptian just as the Egyptian had beaten the Hebrew and ended up killing the Egyptian and hid the dead body in the sand.

The next day he saw two Hebrew brothers fighting with one another and confronted them, asking them why they were fighting. Does this sound familiar? Black on black crime, rival gang wars, drive by shootings? The Hebrews asked Moses if he was their judge and questioned if he was going to kill them like he had killed the Egyptian the day before. He was afraid and knew that the news had gotten out and worried that Pharaoh would have him killed so he ran away to the land of Midian. While he was seated beside a well, the daughters of the priest of Midian came to the well to get water for their father's flock. While that was happening, a group of shepherds also came to the well and forced the flocks away, but Moses came to the daughters' rescue and watered the flocks for them. The women went back home to their father Jethro and told him that an Egyptian had saved them from being bullied by these shepherds. He sent them back to find Moses and told them to invite him over to eat. Moses ends up moving in with them and marrying one of the daughters, Zipporah.

Moses escapes death again. God had a plan for him. All of his experiences, setbacks, connections and knowledge prepares him for his assignment to lead his people out of the land of Egypt. After Egypt's king dies, the Israelites continue to be kept in slavery and begin to cry out to God. He heard their groaning and he remembered the covenant he made with Abraham, Isaac and Jacob. While Moses was tending flock an angel of the LORD appeared to him in flames of fire from within a bush. Moses saw that although the bush was on fire it did not burn up.

> **The LORD said, 'I have indeed seen the misery of my people in Egypt. I have heard them crying out because of their slave drivers, and I am concerned about their suffering. So I have come down to rescue them from the hand of the Egyptians and to bring them up out of that land into a good and spacious land, a land flowing with milk and honey...' (Exodus 3:7-8).**

Moses questioned his ability to lead the Israelites out of Egypt. He made up so many excuses why he couldn't do it. He claimed the people would ask him who sent him, and that they wouldn't believe him, or listen to him. God told Moses to take the staff he had in his hand and to throw it on the ground. When he did, the staff turned into a snake. Moses ran away terrified. God then told him to grab the snake by the tail and when he did, the snake turned back into a staff. Moses was still hesitant so God told him to put his hand in his cloak and take it back out. When he did, his hand turned white like snow, and when he put his hand back in his cloak again, it turned back to normal. God told Moses to show the people the first sign and then the second if they still didn't believe him. He also told Moses if they didn't believe the second sign to take some water from the Nile River, pour it on the ground and it would become blood.

Even after all that, Moses still doubted himself and doubted that the Lord would do what He said He would do. Are we like that? After blessings upon blessings upon blessings; miracles upon miracles upon miracles, we still doubt the power of God. I'm thankful to God that He is a promise keeper! Then Moses asked God to use someone else because he had a stutter. But instead, God decided to send Aaron with him to speak for him. Moses took his wife and sons, put them on a donkey and started back to Egypt with the staff of God in his hand. The LORD told Moses to perform, before Pharaoh, all the wonders he had given him the power to do, but he also told him that he would harden Pharaoh's heart so that he would not let the people go. I will harden his heart so that he will not let the people go.

One detail of this story that I had not studied or understood before writing this book was that on their way to meet Pharaoh, Moses, his wife and his son stopped at a lodging place, and the Lord was about to kill Moses. Before He did, Zipporah, Moses' wife, cut off her son's foreskin—in other words—circumcised him and touched Moses' feet with it. She said, "Surely you are a bridegroom of blood to me." (Exodus 4:26). The Lord then let Moses live. Why would God call Moses to lead His people out of Egypt, then kill him on his way to do exactly what He had commanded him to do?

Dr. Eli Lizorkin-Eyzenberg (2022) academic dean at the Israel Institute of Biblical Studies and the Israel Bible Center suggests that the passage teaches that Moses had not been fully circumcised according to the Abrahamic covenant, likely because he was raised in Egypt and in Pharaoh's household. As Moses prepared to lead Israel out of bondage, he and his son still lacked the covenant sign. God confronted Moses over this, but His wrath was turned away when Moses' son was circumcised, and the covenant blood was applied.

Thank God that today, as Christians, we are covered by the shedding of Jesus blood on Calvary. The blood of Jesus provides protection, covers sins, gives us access to God the Father, among other blessings like healing, authority, deliverance and redemption.

The LORD told Aaron to go meet Moses at the mountain of God and kissed him. Moses told Aaron everything the LORD had sent him to do and say, and about all the signs he had commanded him to perform. Moses and Aaron brought all the elders together and performed the signs before the people, and they believed. When they heard that the LORD was concerned about them and had seen their misery, they bowed down and worshiped. Afterward Moses and Aaron went to Pharaoh and said, "This is what the LORD, the God of Israel, says: 'Let my people go, so that they may hold a festival to me in the wilderness.'" (Exodus 5:1)

That same day Pharaoh ordered the slave drivers to not supply the Israelites with straw to make bricks, but to make them gather their own stray. But they were still required to produce the same number of bricks as before. The work became so hard that Moses asked the Lord why He had brought trouble to the people. Then the Lord said to Moses, "Now you will see what I will do to Pharaoh." (Exodus 6:1). Then the ten plaques of Egypt were sent by God to punish Pharaoh for refusing to let the Israelites leave Egypt. The ten plaques were water turning to blood, frogs, lice, flies, livestock pestilence, boils, hail, locusts, darkness and the killing of firstborn sons. After the tenth plague when the firstborn sons were killed, Pharaoh finally lets the Israelites go. But as we know, Pharaoh pursues them with his army.

When Pharaoh let the people go, God did not lead them on the road through the Philistine country, which was a shorter route. But God led the people around by the desert road toward the Red Sea. As Pharaoh's army drew closer, God told Moses to raise his staff and stretch out his hand over the sea to divide the water so that the Israelites can go through the sea on dry ground. When Moses stretched out his hand over the sea, the LORD drove the sea back with a strong east wind and turned it into dry land. The waters were divided, and the Israelites went through the sea on dry ground, with a wall of water on their right and on their left. The Egyptians pursued them, and all Pharaoh's horses and chariots and horsemen followed them into the sea.

During the last watch of the night, the LORD looked down from the pillar of fire and cloud at the Egyptian army and threw it into confusion. He jammed the wheels of their chariots so that they had difficulty driving. And the Egyptians said, "Let us flee from the face of Israel; for the LORD fighteth for them against the Egyptians" (Exodus 14:25). Then the LORD told Moses to stretch his hand back over the sea and the water flowed back and covered the chariots and horsemen— the entire army of Pharaoh that had followed the Israelites into the sea. Not one of them survived.

Just like Moses was put in that basket as an infant, many are born into boxes of oppression just because of the color of their skin, nationality, socio-economic status or disability. I want to refer back to my earlier statement that the majority often try to solidify power by singling out a perceived weak minority or outsider group and calling them the enemy. In fact, it is fear that usually drives oppression, racism and discrimination. There are so many examples to illustrate this theory.

When we look at the African American experience, the Native American experience and the Holocaust experience, all of these demonstrate a group in power—in an attempt to maintain power—embark oppression upon another group of people.

African Americans were taken from their home, brought over in ships, made slaves, forced to take on the names of their oppressors and robbed of their freedom and humanity. Jews were imprisoned in concentration camps, starved, gassed and massacred in horrific numbers in order to maintain power and dominance. The Native Americans were forced off of their land, made victims of infection and disease and forced to live on reservations, and unjustly culturally assimilated within a culture that was not their own.

For the sake of this writing, I will focus on the African American (Black) experience as it is one that I have the most knowledge of and personal experience with. Even in 2024, Blacks are born into a box. Yes, there are many successful, educated, powerful Blacks in this country. But the number of Blacks is disproportionately represented in terms of arrests, convictions and incarceration. According to Mass Incarceration: The Whole Pie by Wendy Sawyer and Peter Wagner (2004):

- Percent of Black Americans in the general U.S. population: 13% +
- Percent of people in prison or jail who are Black: 37% +
- Prison incarceration rate for Native people vs nation as a whole: 763 vs. 350 per 100,000
- Percent of people serving life, life without parole, or "virtual life" sentences who are Black: 48% +
- Arrest rate for Black vs White Americans: 6.109 vs 2.795 per 100,000+
- Number of arrests of Black Americans in 2018: 2.8 million +
- Percent of people on probation or parole who are Black: 30% +

According to the Mass Incarceration: The Whole Pie 2024, college completion rates of Black students are lower than those of any other ethnic or racial group: 34 percent of Black Americans have an associate degree or higher, compared with 46 percent of the general population. The study is based on a survey that asked more than 6,000 currently enrolled students—including 1,106 Black students—about the challenges they face in higher ed that make degree completion difficult. The survey found that Black students are far more likely to experience racial discrimination than their non-Black peers, and those enrolled at less diverse institutions reported experiencing discrimination more often.

It also found that Black students are more likely than any other group to have a full-time job or significant family caregiving and wage-earning responsibilities—factors that they indicated make it difficult to succeed in college. Black college students have lower six-year college completion rates than any other demographic. A new survey found that cost and discrimination are largely to blame. (Knox, 2022).

For example, Black individuals made up 20.1% of the population in poverty in 2022 but only 13.5% of the total population. This results in a ratio of 1.5, meaning that the Black population was overrepresented in poverty. (US Census Bureau, 2023).

An article from The National Library of Medicine, Inequities in Community Exposure to Deadly Gun Violence by Race/Ethnicity, Poverty, and Neighbourhood Disadvantage among Youth in Large US Cities, "Black and Latinx youth were 3–7 times more likely, depending on the exposure radius, to experience a past-year gun homicide than white youth and on average experienced incidents more recently and closer to home." (J Urban Health, 2022).

Household poverty contributed to exposure inequities, but disproportionate residence in disadvantaged neighbourhoods was especially consequential: for all racial/ethnic groups, the difference in the probability of exposure between youth in low vs high poverty households was approximately 5–10 percentage points, while the difference between youth residing in low vs high disadvantage neighbourhoods was approximately 50 percentage points. Given well-documented consequences of gun violence exposure on health, these more comprehensive estimates underscore the importance of supportive strategies not only for individual victims but entire communities in the aftermath of gun violence.

Looking back to the story of Moses, Pharaoh ordered the death of male babies, similarly to how black males are targeted today. Is the country ordering the death of young black males? Of course not, but the obstacles put in front of them, along with institutionalized racism attributes to their destruction and death. In comparing Pharaoh's decree vs. the mass incarceration of black men, **Pharaoh's goal wasn't random cruelty**—he feared the growing Hebrew population and wanted to weaken their strength and stability. Mass incarceration of Black men in the U.S. has been shown by many scholars to act as a mechanism that disproportionately limits the social, economic, and political power of Black communities. While not identical in intent or method, both function as systems that remove men from their families and communities, weakening those communities' long-term strength. Both target the group's future. Both flow from free-based power. Both are maintained through institutional power.

When we look at Moses' story, we see a God who steps into impossible situations with purpose, protection, and destiny. And that same God still intervenes today—especially in the life of any Black man who chooses to trust Him, seek Him, and surrender his path to Him. Moses could have stayed a fugitive. He could have let his past define him. But God's call was bigger than his mistakes. Many Black men carry burdens from childhood, trauma, missteps, or societal labels. But when they trust God, He lifts them above every identity the world tries to place on them. He calls them to lead families, communities, ministries, and nations.

12 CONSTRUCTING BOARDERS

The eighth way to get in a box is by building our own box and stepping into it. Being bound in a box is not always a bad thing. Sometimes a box can serve as a shield of protection or a temporary place of rest and rebirth. I want to share two biblical examples of building your own box. The first story I want to look at is the story of Noah and the ark. The art that housed Noah and his family was a box of protection. According to Genesis 6, the descendants of Adam and Eve had become evil and wicked, and God was sorry He had ever created mankind. He decided the only thing to do was destroy them all and start over! But there was one man, Noah, who was obedient to God and found God's favour. God told Noah to build a big boat, called an *ark*, and He told Noah exactly how to do it. The ark was to be 450 ft. (137 m) long, 75 ft. (23 m) wide and 45 ft. (14 m) high. It was to have three decks, be divided into rooms and have a door in the side.

Noah was to find one male and one female of every kind of animal and bird and take them into the ark. He also had to take food for all those animals. It took Noah 120 years to build the ark and find all the animals to put in it, but Noah obeyed God and did just as he was told.

Noah was 600 years old by the time everything was ready. God told Noah to go into the ark with his wife, his three sons, Shem, Ham, and Japheth, and their wives. Then it started to rain. It rained without stop for forty days and nights! The water got so deep that even the mountains were covered. Every living creature on earth died in the flood. But the ark floated on top of the flood waters and the people and animals in the ark were safe.

Eventually, the water started to go down again, and the ark came to rest in the mountains of Ararat. After being on the ark about 11 months, Noah sent out a dove to see if it would find land, but it found no place to rest and returned to the ark. Seven days later, Noah sent the dove out again. This time it flew back carrying an olive leaf, and Noah knew it had found land. After a full year on the ark, God said to Noah,

> **Come out of the ark, you and your wife and your sons and their wives. Bring out every kind of living creature that is with you – the birds, the animals, and all the creatures that move along the ground – so they can multiply on the earth and be fruitful and increase in number upon it. (Genesis 8:16-17, NIV).**

After leaving the ark, Noah built an altar and worshipped God. God was pleased with Noah, and He promised never again to destroy the earth with a flood. Then God placed a rainbow in the sky as a sign of that promise. The descendants of Noah and his sons filled the whole earth with people again. Except for Noah and his family, all the people of the world were going about their evil and wicked ways. The earth was filled with violence. Mankind had lost sight of God and the way He wanted them to live together in harmony. God rewarded Noah for his righteousness, but He decided there was no choice but to destroy the wicked people of the earth.

When God placed Noah and his family inside the ark, He wasn't just giving them a boat—He was placing them in a divinely crafted box of protection. While the world around them was falling apart, the ark became a safe, sealed space where God preserved their lives, their purpose, and their future. It was a box designed not to confine them, but to carry them through a season of destruction they were never meant to face. Inside that box, God sheltered them from the storm, from judgment, and from everything that had the power to wipe them out.

The ark represents how God sometimes places His people in enclosed, unfamiliar, uncomfortable spaces—not to limit them, but to protect, prepare, and preserve them until the storm passes. When the waters receded and the door opened, Noah stepped out not into confinement but into a new beginning. The ark shows us that God's "boxes" are never prisons—they are temporary places of safety until it's time to walk into what He has prepared next.

The second example of building your own box and entering into it is the story of Jesus in the Garden of Gethsemane. According to Matthew 26:36-46, Jesus went to the Garden of Gethsemane to pray. Jesus went with his disciples to a place called Gethsemane, and he asked them to sit at wait while he went away to pray. Jesus took Peter and the two sons of Zebedee along with him, and he became very sad and troubled. Jesus went on to say that his soul was overwhelmed to the point of death. I am only imagine feeling so overwhelmed where death feels like comfort because all you want is to escape from the reality you are facing and only in death will you truly escape. I know for many that are overwhelmed with anxiety, depression, or guilt see death as their own means of escape. According to the American Association of Suicidology (2009), the risk of suicide in people with major depression is about 20 times that of the general population.

The Bible says that Jesus fell with His face to the ground and prayed. He asked God if it was possible to take the *cup* away from Him—that is, the suffering He was about to face. But He also said that if it wasn't possible, He wanted God's will to be done, not His own.

Jesus experienced human emotions and even asked God to remove his from the painful experience he was about to endure, but as we know, God did not, but God did give him the strength to endure and accomplish the task given to him. God gave him the strength. He may have felt alone and forsaken, but the garden was actually a place to focus to gain strength in preparation for what was to come.

Sometime situations we must face or decisions we must make, cause extreme anxiety, but we know we have to do it. It may be for our own good or for the good of others. Not comparing our situations with those of Jesus who gave his own life and shed his blood for the sins of the world, but situations, nevertheless are dreadful to us. The crucifixion of Jesus was prophesized in the book of Isaiah.

> **He was oppressed and afflicted, yet he did not open his mouth; he was led like a lamb to the slaughter, and as a sheep before its shearers is silent, so he did not open his mouth. (Isaiah 53:7).**

In the book of John, when it was almost time for the Jewish Passover, Jesus went up to Jerusalem and found people in the temple courts he found people selling cattle, sheep and doves, and others sitting at tables exchanging money. Jesus was so angry that he made a whip out of cords and overturned their tables and kicked them all out. The Jews asked him to show them a sign to prove that he had authority to kick people out of the temple and to knock the tables over. Jesus responded by telling them if the temple was destroyed, He would raise it again in three days.

Although they thought Jesus was talking about the physical temple, Jesus was talking about His resurrection. Jesus knew it had been prophesized and he knew what his assignment was, but still he asked God if the cup could pass by him. In other words, the fact that he was all God, he was also all man. He was afraid because he knew he was facing torture and death. However, he also knew he had to follow through so that prophesy would be fulfilled and to save all of us. He was the ultimate sacrificial lamb. Jesus' box was his Gethsemane. It was his quiet place to get close to God, to speak with God, to pour out his hear to God, to express his fear, but also be regain the strength he needed to fulfill his mission.

Often times we have to find our Gethsemane. We have to create our box—our quiet place to commune with God. Some of us go into a physical prayer closet. Some of us separate ourselves from friends and family who don't understand what our calling is. Some of us separate ourselves from bad habits or sin that held us bound. Some of us have to cut some people out of our lives in order to move forward with God and walk in our purpose. Whatever your Gethsemane is, when we need to build that box and walk in that box, we need to do it so we can walk out of that box stronger.

13 THE QUIET PULL INTO SMALL SPACES

The ninth way a box surrounds us is sometimes it forms around us without anyone causing it—life just builds it piece by piece. There are seasons when you find yourself surrounded by a box you never created and no one else intended. These boxes aren't the result of blame—they simply appear around you as life unfolds.

As we look at the story of the prophet Jeremiah, referred to as "The Weeping Prophet." Jeremiah was very young when God placed a heavy call on his life. The verse is Jeremiah 1:5, which states: "Before I formed you in the womb I knew you, before you were born I set you apart; I appointed you as a prophet to the nations". This verse is a message from God to Jeremiah, explaining that God knew him and had a specific purpose for his life even before his birth. Jeremiah felt unprepared and too inexperienced because he was so young. God responded by assuring Jeremiah that He was chosen and that He promised to be with him and to give him the words he needed. From that moment on, Jeremiah walked a path very few would ever understand.

Unfortunately, Jeremiah was a prophet no one wanted to hear. Jeremiah carried messages that weren't easy to deliver—warnings about the nation's sin, calls to repent, and predictions of coming judgment. Instead of listening, the people laughed at him, mocked him, and refused to believe his words. Leaders tried to silence him, priests rejected him, and even his own neighbors plotted against him. It's one thing to be rejected by strangers. But Jeremiah experienced rejection from the very people he loved the most. That type of rejection from the people you expect to love you and protect you at all costs is the most painful abandonment to experience.

Some of Jeremiah's deepest wounds came from friends and family who turned their backs on him. They whispered about him behind closed doors, hoping to catch him slipping so they could accuse him. He felt surrounded by people waiting to see him fail. Jeremiah's own family and townspeople in Anathoth plotted to kill him. The men of Anathoth are quoted saying, "You must not prophesy in the name of the LORD, or you will die by our hand" (Jeremiah 11:19-21).

Jeremiah describes himself as "like a lamb led to the slaughter," unaware of their plans until the Lord revealed them. He recounts their desire to "destroy the tree with its fruit," a metaphor for eradicating both him and his prophetic message. (Jeremiah 11:19). And yet, every time he wanted to quit, something inside him kept burning. He said God's word felt like fire in his bones—too strong to ignore, even when it hurt.

Jeremiah's ministry was filled with loneliness, sorrow, and emotional exhaustion. He cried for his people. He questioned God at times. He even wondered why his life had to be so hard. There were moments when Jeremiah felt depressed, overwhelmed, and tired of carrying burdens that weren't his own. Jeremiah wrote honestly about his heartbreak, isolation, insults, and the pressure of speaking truth when on one wanted to hear it.

For years, Jeremiah had been warning the people of Judah that danger was approaching. Babylon was rising in power, and Jeremiah—speaking God's message—told the nation that if they didn't turn back to God, their city would fall. But the leaders didn't want to hear it. By the time we reach Jeremiah 38, Babylon had surrounded Jerusalem. Food was running out. Fear was running high. Everyone wanted good news, even if it wasn't true. But Jeremiah kept speaking the truth—telling everyone that the city would fall and that the king would be captured, but if they would surrender, they would love. This message did not make Jeremiah popular.

Four powerful officials—Shephatiah, Gedaliah, Jehucal, and Pashhur—felt Jeremiah's words were dangerous. They believed he was lowering the morale of the soldiers, discouraging the people, weakening the nation, and helping the enemy by telling people not to fight. To them, Jeremiah wasn't a prophet—he was a threat. They went to King Zedekiah and told him that Jeremiah must be put to death. Before being thrown in a pit, he was beaten, imprisoned, an interrogated, but he continued to prophesy exactly what God had told him.

When Jeremiah kept speaking the same message from prison, the officials grew more furious. In their minds, the only way to shut him up was to remove him completely. But they didn't want to execute him because they thought it would make them directly responsible. Instead, they threw him in a muddy pit.

Was Jeremiah resentful? Yes, but not in the sense of wanting revenge or turning bitter toward God—but he did struggle with deep frustration, hurt, and honest complaints. His emotions were real, raw, and sometimes intense. Jeremiah expressed the plea, "Why is my pain unending and my wound grievous and incurable?" (Jeremiah 15:18). At times, Jeremiah asked God to deal with those who were trying to destroy him. Jeremiah cries out to God, "O LORD, You know; remember me and visit me, and take vengeance for me on my persecutors" (Jeremiah 15:15).

The Bible preserves his prayers so we can see how human he truly was. Jeremiah proved to be a faithful man. He walked through rejection, betrayal, and deep sorrow, yet held onto God so tightly that even his tears became a testimony of trust. Jeremiah carried his calling—and the pain that came with it—for his entire ministry. He never had a "breakthrough moment" where everything suddenly stopped hurting. The rejection, loneliness, and mistreatment didn't magically disappear. He was faithful, but he was still human.

Through it all, Jeremiah trusted God. Even though the pain didn't go away, Jeremiah learned to bring his complaints to God and to trust God's justice instead of seeking his own. Jeremiah's greatest turning point wasn't emotional relief—it was spiritual confidence. In Lamentations 3 he says,

> **This I recall to my mind, therefore have I hope. It is of the LORD's mercies that we are not consumed, because his compassions fail not. They are new every morning: great is thy faithfulness. The LORD is my portion, saith my soul; therefore will I hope in him. (Lamentations 3: 21-24).**

Jeremiah lived in a box that he never asked for, but because God lived there with him, the box became a place of purpose, strength, and unbreakable hope.

14 ABOUT THE BOX

When I think about a box, I picture a shoebox or large cardboard box that refrigerators are packaged in, but there are so many more different types of boxes as I shared earlier. Boxes are made of different materials and some are more difficult to penetrate than others. Just like the boxes we find ourselves in, some of them are harder for us to escape from. Some are even impossible to escape from without the help of someone else or without divine intervention. Not only are boxes different sizes and made from different materials, boxes are also different in their appearance. Metal, for example, is shinier than wood, plastic, and cardboard. Sometimes boxes in our lives appear shiny to us, or attractive to the eye, and it's not until we realize we are trapped, that we understand the shininess was simply a ploy.

I know we've all heard the proverb, "The grass is always greener on the other side." But if we dare to ask why the grass is greener, we might find that someone on the other side is actually watering the grass, digging up weeds and feeding the grass proper nutrients. How much greener would our grass be if we just watered it, pulled up our weeds and didn't allow others to walk through it. Apparent boxes visually look like they are easy to escape from because we can see through them, that is until you attempt to break free, and then you realize that the plastic wall, although apparent, is thick and hard to cut into and through.

The security of boxes is also different. Cardboard boxes are usually taped together on at least one side, which would make it easier to open than say a steel box which has been welded together, as we looked at earlier. Wood boxes may have small openings in them where the wood was either glued together or nailed together. Thus, when you look at the different types of situations some of them may be easier to break free from than others. You may be able to bust out of some with one quick punch or kick, like the example of a paper box (resisting and he will flee from you), but others might require gradually picking yourself out starting with a small crack or opening (prayer and fasting), and still others might require some help from someone on the outside of the box (discernment and intercession) or even the supernatural (divine intervention).

Finally, we must realize that boxes never end. What I mean by that, is as we grow spiritually, the boxes become more challenging, but from each box, we take knowledge gained and learn to deal with new situations as they occur. We are able to identify when we have entered a box quicker and learn new ways and techniques to escape from them. I believe that each new box that we successfully escape from, represents a test that we have successfully passed. And God pays attention to every victory and to how we navigate each "box" we face. Through our responses, He determines what He can trust us with and what roles or responsibilities He will place in our hands in these last days. As Scripture warns, "Now the Spirit speaketh expressly, that in the latter times some shall depart from the faith, giving heed to seducing spirits, and doctrines of devils." (1 Timothy 4:1)

OUT OF THE BOX

When you finally realize it, what a revelation! You know sometimes I believe that we, meaning believers, start off by doing something that the Lord has prompted us to do, but by no fault of our own, we end up way off base and out in left field. Other times, we willingly step right off a base where we're safe and venture out into the unknown outside of the safety of God, opening ourselves to consequences, whatever those might be. "Yea, and all that will live godly in Christ Jesus shall suffer persecution. But continue thou in the things which thou hast learned and hast been assured of, knowing of whom thou hast learned them." (II Timothy 3:12,14)

Let's use a baseball example; A player, new to the game of baseball, is told to play second base or third base, but somehow ended up playing in the outfield, causing the runner on first base of the opposing team to get to second base and the runner on second to proceed to third. For me, I felt stuck in the outfield like that baseball player, without any training and I wasn't sure if the Lord wanted me to stay out in the field, move back to second base, or first, or run to the dugout and sit and watch the other players. Well, I wasn't certain so I stayed in the outfield until the coach, the Lord Himself, clearly and loudly, but ever so gently said, "Now it's time to come off the field."

I still did not know what position if any I was to play, but I knew without any doubt that the Lord had made the call for me to get off the field and wait for further instructions. It seemed that I had waited an eternity, but a thousand years is as a day with the Lord. (II Peter 3:8) And what a great day this was. A day in which the box which had my mind and my body sealed was opened ever so gently without a rip or tear. I crawled out of this box, barely able to stand, and gradually was able to stand again, then walk and finally run. But just when I thought

I had it all figured out, I was back in another box, this time a stronger box with stronger seals. But through it all, I learned how great God's grace and mercy are. Psalm 103:4 tells us that God redeems us from life's destructions and crowns us with loving kindness and tender mercies. For me, God began to reveal a lifetime of boxes that I experiences and the lessons I learned from each box.

When it appears in the natural that your life is being destroyed and that Satan has robbed you of your joy, take comfort in knowing that the Lord will never leave you or forsake you. And Philippians 4:6-7 teaches us not to worry about anything, but to pray with thanksgiving and let our request be known unto God, and the peace of God, which we do not understand, will guard our hearts and mind through Christ Jesus.

Our faith and trust in Jesus Christ guard our hearts and minds from being overtaken and overpowered by the enemy. As believers, we will be tried and tested. Sometimes to the point where we feel like giving up, but our hearts and minds are guarded. Isn't this great news. What we truly believe and hide in our heart is shielded and our minds are protected from takeover. The enemy may invade our heart and mind, and even get us focusing on the negative, but he won't be able to take over because we have the greater one working on the inside of us guarding us and keeping us in dangers seen and unseen. Often times we don't even realize that we are treading in dangerous waters; sometimes a calm and tranquil stream flows into a rushing river, but God is and always will be "The Life Saver." I know He saved mine!

15 THE EARLY DAYS

I have often looked back over my life and been able to pick out specific circumstances where the Lord had guarded my heart and mind from takeover. Upon writing this book, I have discovered that there are key defining moments in my life that I now identity and label as Box Experiences. Through each of those Box Experiences, my God—the God of Abraham, Isaac and Jacob; the Lord Jesus Christ and the Greatest Comforter, the Holy Spirit was there and always delivered me Out of the Box, time and time again.

Young children are very trusting, forgiving, and committed to those whom they love. I can remember my elementary school years and wanting to tell everybody about Jesus. I had no shame: I was a bold and confident witness for Christ. My brother and I grew up in the church. My mom took us to Sunday school every Sunday and taught us right from wrong at a very early age. My dad did not go to church regularly, but he was the best representative of what goodness and kindness was. We were taught to trust in God for everything. And as children, we did! If mommy said, "This is what the Bible says," then it was so. Living for Jesus was all we knew.

OUT OF THE BOX

One of my fondest memories was sitting around the TV on New Years' Day 1973 watching The Ohio State Buckeyes vs. The USC Trojans in The Rose Bowl. My mom had prepared Sauerkraut—as she always had. It was a tradition—one that I looked forward to. Why was this football game so significant? The 1973 Rose Bowl was the first time Ohio State's first starting Black quarterback, Cornelius Greene, started a game for the Buckeyes. The quarterback position had traditionally always been played by a white player. Due to "racial stacking" in sports, in which players are typecast into certain on-field positions based on racial stereotypes, Black players were rarely granted opportunities as quarterbacks, as it was considered a "thinking" position. I saw the look of joy and pride on the faces of my mom, dad, and uncle, who normally came over to watch the games with us.

The idea of racial inequalities never entered my mind at such a young age, yet I knew that day, a change had occurred. I had not been directly exposed to racism and didn't know that my being black and a woman meant living at the intersection of race and gender. These pressures often overlap, creating experiences that are different from those of Black men *or* non-Black women. Today, scholars call it *intersectionality*—but Black women have lived it long before it had a name.

As a child, I remember walking to the bus stop early Sunday morning, riding the bus downtown and transferring in front of what was then, Lazarus, and hopping on the westbound bus to our church on the West side, on S. Eureka Avenue in Columbus, Ohio. Our family only had one car at the time and my dad worked most Sundays so my mom, brother and I took the bus to church. I remember a young woman from the church was always waiting at the same bus stop

Sunday morning after our first transfer. Sunday School was a must and after learning bible stories in church, I couldn't wait to share those stories with other kids on the playground at school.

Another memory is sitting around on the playground in elementary school talking with my friends about Jesus, Heaven and Hell. Instead of playing tether ball or foursquare, which were the popular games in my early childhood, my friends and I would find a nice shade tree and lay back and talk. We had some very in-depth conversations. We talked about boys, sex, drugs, alcohol, smoking and other topics too numerous to mention. We made promises to each other about not being taken in by the world and what the world stands for. We talked about waiting until marriage to have sex, about never smoking or drinking, and living holy.

Now when I look back on those years, I see how blessed I was to be surrounded by friends who believed the same way I did at an early age. The Lord was guarding my heart and mind from being polluted and conformed to this world. The faith that was instilled in me at home was able to grow without being uprooted. I knew that Jesus was able to heal my body, supply my needs, and empower me to be an overcomer. No questions asked: it was just simple faith, childlike faith, kingdom faith. I suppose this is what Jesus meant when He said, "Verily I say unto you, Whosoever shall not receive the kingdom of God as a little child, he shall not enter therein" (Mark: 10:15).

Even though I loved the Lord and trusted Him with the knowledge and understanding of a child, it was just that, childlike faith. As children we easily trust what others tell us, especially those who are close to us, and we accept God's word on simple faith. Although this is true, there comes a time in our life when we move from milk to meat. We grow from not simply believing God's word, to truly understanding what his Word means and why it is so important for our daily living. My mom used to quote this particular scripture to me all the time from Proverbs 4: 7 which states: "Wisdom is the principle thing; therefore, get wisdom: and with all thy getting, get understanding." I didn't comprehend what the scripture actually meant, but I knew it had something to do with making sure you understood whatever someone was telling you.

Understanding is so important, and I know this now. We must come to understand, not just in our minds, but in our heart and spirit. Why God's word says this or that about any principle: it's the *why* that helps us to understand and to want to accept it. When I was in third grade, I had a very weak bladder. I couldn't go all night without wetting the bed. I remember my third-grade teacher, Ms. Lester, invited all the girls in my class to spend the night at her house. Ms. Lester was a young black female teacher, probably straight out of college who was more than just a teacher to her students. When I asked my mom if I could spend the night, she immediately, without even thinking about it, said, "No." I was so hurt and upset. I didn't understand; I felt that she was just being mean. She tried to explain to me that I still had accidents at night, and that she didn't want me to be embarrassed, but I didn't get it. I didn't care; I just wanted to go. Now as an adult I understand that her love for me was so strong that she didn't want me to feel the pain from the other children teasing me. Why she wouldn't allow me to go was far more important than the fact that I couldn't go.

Likewise, God's Word, especially when it concerns issues of morality and His will for our life can best be understood when we get to the *why?* God's Word is very clear in terms of moral behavior. God loves us so much that He, through His Word or the Holy Spirit tells us what we can or cannot do and still remain in God's will and under the shadow of the Almighty. And since man is made in the likeness of God, then when we have difficulties with things or problems overcoming certain strongholds, we need to look at the word, and first of all find out what the word says about it, and pray to the Lord for an understanding of why this is God's will, and finally why this is happening in our life. I've heard it said before, "don't question the Lord." And I'm not suggesting we question Him, but get an understanding from Him and get to know Him—what He thinks, and what He feels. I don't claim to be a Bible expert, or even one who has a special revelation from God. All I know is that throughout my life, I have found myself time and time again, getting trapped in boxes, and not knowing how I got in them or how to get out. And it wasn't until I was at my lowest and sought the Lord for revelation knowledge as to why, that I grew to understand why, and eventually learned that I could be free and stay free.

One incident happened to me in the third grade, which I consider my earliest memory of being in a box. I guess third grade was a testing year for me. Every day, this little boy, who will remain nameless, used to chase me home and threaten to beat me up. I'll never forget him. He actually reached out to me over 20 years ago when *Myspace* first entered the scene. I asked him why he tormented me in the third grade. Of course, he had no memory of it, but he did apologize for how he treated me. There are times when we experience hurt and pain and sometimes that pain stays with us for years. While at the same time, those individuals who caused us pain have moved on with their lives, not even remembering their actions or recognizing that their actions had an effect on someone else.

Back to my story, on certain days, while still in class, this boy would whisper to me that he was going to "get me" when the bell rang. I was a very fast runner, so I would grab my things, and run to the restroom crying with fear. I would stay in there long enough for my face to regain its color. The other kids nicknamed me Rudolph that year because my nose would get really red when I was crying, and it was difficult to hide it, especially from people who knew me well. So, after I came out of the restroom, most of the children had already gone home, and I ran as fast as I could all the way home. When I got home, my mother was always waiting for me. She would ask me, "DuBonna, how was your day?" I would tell her that it was good, but of course it wasn't. I was in a box.

I held that fear and pain inside for weeks until finally one day, when I made it home, my nose was still red. I guess I hadn't hidden in the bathroom at school long enough for my nose to regain its color. My mother knew something was wrong. I couldn't keep it any longer. I told her everything; I told her how this boy would chase me home and block the sidewalk so I couldn't get past and threaten to "kick my butt". The very next morning, she took me to class and told my teacher what had been going on. Ms. Lester couldn't believe that I didn't trust her enough to tell her so she could have handled it. After Mrs. Lester talked with this little boy, called his parents, and made him stay after school for detention for a week, which allowed me to get a head start for home, he never threatened me or chased me home again. That box is minuscule, compared to future boxes that I found myself in, but at the time, it was devastating. For me, the way I was able to escape from that box was the support of my mother and my teacher.

Mrs. Lester explained to me that sometimes little boys don't know how to express their feelings about little girls, therefore, when a boy has a crush on a girl, he teases her or harasses her. It's his way of getting her attention—any way that he can. That answered my question of why he bothered me, but why didn't I speak out? Why did I try to hide a serious problem that I was having and try to deal with in myself and not trust someone close to me help me solve it? After all, Ms. Lester was a wonderful teacher. I knew she would have understood, and I knew she would have dealt with my problem, but still I said nothing. Well, nothing until I was backed into a box with only one way out. And if my mom had not seen my red nose, I wouldn't have spoken up. This particular box had me bound in fear and kept me focused on what was in the box—a way to get home without being caught and without my mom noticing my red nose.

I allowed myself to be continuously harassed by this little boy and confined to that box of torment when all I needed to do was open it up. All I needed to do was to *speak up*. I guess this is why I ask my children and grandchildren so many questions now. I don't ever want them to feel that they cannot come to me and tell me anything. I recall telling my youngest daughter years ago, "No matter what you do, I'll always love you." One day she asked me, "Mom, will you always love me no matter what I do." I told her, "Yes," and she just smiled. She just needed to make sure. One day my son, when he was about four years old asked me, "Do you love your little son?" And naturally I told him yes. Then he asked me, "What if someone kidnapped me? How would you feel?" I told him that if someone stole him, I would have to go to the hospital. He wanted to know how I would end up in the hospital if he was stolen? I explained to him that I loved him so much that if he was taken from my life, I would be so sick that I wouldn't be able to function, so I know God will never allow that to happened. I wanted him to know how much I loved him, but that God loves him even more, and that he can trust Him with all their problems, and all their secrets because He knows them anyway and He loves him in spite of them.

I am in no way saying that my parents didn't communicate with me as a child because they did. They were both very active and interested in my spiritual, educational, social, and emotional development. They always supported me and were there to back me when I was in the right. Notice I said when I was in the right. Now if I was wrong, they let me know that also. I'll tell you about one of those incidents later. So back to why I kept it all inside. I suppose it was fear, but fear of what? Fear comes in so many different forms. Fear attaches itself to individuals.

For some it may be the fear of rejection or for others it may be the fear of disappointing other people, or the fear of being harassed even more. There are so many; too many to name. But neither of those reasons applied to me. I didn't care if the little boy rejected me; actually, I wanted him to totally reject me. I didn't care if I disappointed him, and I didn't fear that he wouldn't't be my friend. All I wanted was for him to leave me alone and I wanted to handle it myself. I felt strong enough to do it on my own; I didn't want to bother anyone with it. It was my problem and I thought I could just take it! I believe that deep down inside I was afraid that my speaking up would have a far greater consequence than being taken advantage of every day.

Reflecting back on it now, I was pushed into that box of fear—threatened by that little boy. When faced with fear, I tried ways to protect myself—leaving the classroom a few minutes before the other kids, racing to the bathroom to prepare myself for the run home, and running home as quickly as I could to keep from being caught. But I was also drawn deeper into the box—allowing myself to be controlled by fear. Looking back, as I consider the various materials boxes are made of, I would say that box was made of notebook paper, relatively easy to tear my way out. But as a third grader, that box felt like I was being held hostage in a plastic storage bin—one you can find at any hardware store. I knew there was a way to open it, but I didn't have the strength to pull that top off. It took someone from the outside noticing that something wasn't right. It also took my stepping out of my comfort zone, ripping that paper, and telling my mom what had been going on. Finally, it took my teacher—the person with authority—to take action on my behalf.

Although it's a simple example of the principle of bondage—being under the control of another person, circumstance or spirit—the concept remains the same. Unfortunately, many people accept things in their life that they should not accept. And they allow those things to become strong holds. Satan is a liar and a deceiver, and he convinces us that that's just the way it is! And those things attach themselves to us and then become a familiar spirit—meant to enforce a negative pattern. Just like we know what upsets us and our weaknesses, Satan knows those things as well. He studies our moves; and waits for the attack.

Familiar spirits attach themselves to individuals and follow them around until they are identified, cast out, and not permitted to enter in again. Satan knows the word of God, and he knows who knows the word and who doesn't. He also knows what it takes to get our goat. Like it states in 1 Peter 5:8, "Be sober, be vigilant; because your adversary the devil, as a roaring lion, walketh about, seeking whom he may devour."

My husband is a nature buff. He enjoys watching the animal shows, especially the episodes about the predators. Occasionally I watch shows with him. I have seen for myself that the lion is very sneaky and cunning. He studies his prey before he pounces on them to make the kill. His mission is not to wound his prey; he is out to devour them— to completely destroy any evidence of life. Likewise, Satan is not merely out to wound us or slow us down, he is out to demolish us. Satan comes to steal, kill, and to destroy, but Jesus came that we might have life, and have it more abundantly. The mother gazelle teaches her young to be aware of the enemy at all times; not to worry, but to always stand guard. Joshua 1:9 says: "Have not I commanded thee? Be strong and of a good courage; be not afraid, neither be thou dismayed: for the Lord thy God is with thee whithersoever thou goest."

As a parent, it was important for me to teach my children about the tactics of the enemy and to prepare them for battle and to empower them for the fight. Although the Lord is our refuge and our present help in time of trouble, and he guards our hearts and minds, we have an important part to play in our covering. I'm sure that the majority of Christian adults today have strayed away from the Lord at some point in their life. But there is something about a seed that is planted in good soil, a pure heart, that always grows and produces good fruit. It may take longer for certain flowers to blossom, but the right amount of water and sunlight will produce a plant that is healthy and strong.

Behold a sower went forth to sow; and when he sowed, some seeds fell by the way side, and the fowls came and devoured them up. Some fell upon stony places where they had not much earth; and forthwith they sprung up, because they had no deepness of earth: and when the sun was up, they were scorched; and because they had no root, they withered away. And some fell among thorns; and the thorns sprung up, and choked them. But other fell into good ground, and brought for fruit, some an hundredfold, some sixty fold, some thirty fold" (Matthew 13:3-8).

In fourth grade, I experienced my "Aha Moment." It was the moment I realized that because I was Black, and a black woman, I would be treated differently. I also realized that having money, or coming from a family with money had its advantages, and those who did not, were treated differently.

The summer before entering fourth grade, our family moved from the Linden area in Columbus to Berwick—then considered a middle-class neighborhood with working professionals. In fourth grade, the students were divided into reading groups based on their reading level. In my class at Eleventh Avenue Elementary School, located in the Linden area, I was in the highest-level reading group. I was a straight A student and excelled in all my classes. When we moved to Berwick, I was placed in the lowest reading group, although I didn't realize it at the time. One afternoon after school, my mom asked me how I was doing in class and it just so happened that she asked me about my reading group. I explained that our class had 4 reading groups and I believed I was in the lowest group.

Even though school districts don't come right out and say it, but children are labeled early on and sometimes those labels stay with them throughout high school and graduation. I had been labeled and put in a reading group without being tested simply because of the neighborhood and part of town I came from. I was put in a box after our move, without having done anything to cause it. Likewise, many children today are labeled and not given opportunities because they are systematically labeled and restricted. Fortunately for me, I had a mother who wasn't afraid to ask "why"?

The next week, my mom came up to the school and spoke with my teacher and asked why I had been placed in the lowest reading group. My teacher went on to explain that based on my school records, the next book in that series happened to be the book that the children in the lowest reading group were reading. My mom explained to my teacher that in my former school, I was a straight "A" student and was in the highest group and requested for me to be tested. As it turned out, my teacher was hesitant and my mom had to meet with the principal and some other school officials to give me that opportunity. I remember my mom telling me that the next morning I was going to take a test to make sure I was in the right reading group.

I remember arriving at school very early the next morning, well before the other students arrived, going to a small little room and being asked to sit down next to a very petite elderly woman. I was presented with a book, asked to read it aloud and answer questions about what I had read. She took notes while I was reading and when I was writing. After reading the first book, I was asked to read anther and another. A few days later, on the way to school, I recall my mom saying, "Today, you will be a new reading group." I don't remember anything more or less. I didn't ask questions because I didn't really understand what had taken place, but I figured I had done good on the test. Unfortunately, a lot of kids, young people and adults don't have that one person who is not afraid to ask "why"? The disparity between the school districts was blatantly obvious.

Another Aha moment for me was when I realized that people looked at me differently as a black female, and to some, I wasn't good enough. It was fifth grade, and a group of friends were sitting around class during free time talking about who would make a good couple. Yes, we were talking about couples in the fifth grade. Remember we had moved from a predominately black neighborhood to a neighborhood who was highly populated with Jews. My best friends were Jewish and I hadn't realized we were different until this particular day. Anyways, someone told one of the boys in the classroom, who happened to be Jewish, "You and Dubonna would be a cute couple." He laughed and said, "She's cute, but I can't have a black girlfriend." I didn't like this little boy or any other boy for that reason, but I remember this incident so clearly because that's when I realized that being black was different and undervalued. I didn't know at the time how different, what being black meant, how being black would affect my future, how others would perceive me or what limitations I would face, but I knew instantly that his comment meant something! I was unknowing placed into a box—a box that labeled me as inferior. A double-minority—one being subjected to racism and sexism.

OUT OF THE BOX

Double Minority

Dubonna L Dawkins

A Woman?
Yea…
That's me
Black?
Am I still called that?
African American?
I'm that too!
Do they trust me?
Believe in me?
Fake?
I don't know
I try not to care
They will never understand
If they are not me
Never know
How it feels
To be
Double Minority

16 TESTING THE WATERS

Seeds were planted in my heart as a young child, and the seeds were watered, but it seemed as I grew into adolescence, my faith and my obedience to the word began to change. I continued to love the Lord, but my commitment to Holiness didn't seem as urgent. I don't know if teens feel they need to test their limits, or explore the world, but for me I believe that I always knew what was right and wrong. Nevertheless, the purpose why God called me to Holiness was never truly understood during my adolescence.

I had my share of straying away from the word: the parties, the drinking, the smoking, missing curfew, lying about whose house I was at; maybe some of you have been there? But what is so funny was that if there was an opportunity to talk about Jesus, even if I was at a party that I sneaked to go to, I still had the nerve to call on the name of Jesus. I even had the nerve to witness to some friends about Jesus. I'm sure those same friends were thinking, you're doing the same things that we're doing, so why should we get to know Jesus? What's the point? Jesus was the point; He is still the point, and he's the answer to it all. But so many times we do not represent Him well. Yes, He is the point; He is the answer; He is it all, but how can we convince others that He is it all when we bring shame to the body of Christ.

Even still, after we have shamed Him, grieved Him and quenched Him, He's still it all! When you need a friend, he's there. When you need a doctor, he's there. When you need a lawyer, he's there. When you need to pay a bill, he's there. When you need a place to lay your head, he's there. When you need forgiveness, he's there. I know he was there for me so many times. How good is God's grace? How precious is His love? Even when I was so off base as a young woman, he was still there to allow me to run home safely and receive me like the prodigal son.

Sometimes I try to imagine what the Lord actually says when he looks down on his children and sees them in disobedience. I imagine Him saying, "Why won't they just listen to me, I know what I'm talking about!" I know when I was in high school, my mother used to always tell me, "A good name is rather to be chosen than great riches, and loving favor rather than silver and gold" (Proverbs 22:1).

I know that some of the choices I made were not choices that should have produced a good name, nevertheless, I believe most people considered me a nice and kind person. I know it was only because of the grace of God again. Time and time and time after time again, he showed me such great favor. God's favor describes His gracious kindness and support. It's not something we earn by being perfect—it's something God gives because of His love, purpose, and relationship with us.

Everything I had—every gift; every talent—came from Him. The Lord blessed me with a wonderful talent. I was a really good sprinter in high school. Not sounding boastful, but I was one of the best in the state of Ohio—qualifying to the state meet multiple years. I started running track when I was seven or eight years old, so I had lots of practice, and practice does make perfect. Anyway, at our high school, athletes—especially the talented ones—were really popular, just like at most schools. The popularity is generally due to a combination of social recognition, leadership opportunities, and school spirit. Team members build strong social connections through teamwork and shared experiences, leading to visibility across different social groups. They are also seen as leaders, embodying qualities like discipline, dedication, and a strong sense of school pride. I remember throughout junior high and high school how the morning announcements always highlighted the names of our 400-meter relay team and mile relay team.

Aside from being successful in the sport, I was also a straight "A" student, and a drill team captain, and a Homecoming Queen finalist. I loved the Lord. I know I did. And He surrounded me with very hard-working intelligent peers. I could have been an instrument that the Lord used to lead many to Christ, but I didn't. My friends knew I went to church, but they didn't truly witness a Christ-like lifestyle. So instead of being an evangelist for Jesus, I chose a path that was not so bright. I made some bad choices. I chose the world's way and not the Lord's way. That little girl who gathered friends for Bible studies on the elementary playground—promising together never to drink, smoke, or have sex before marriage—slowly drifted into what the world called normal.

"The grass withers, the flower fades: but the word of our God shall stand for ever" (Isaiah 40:8). No matter what the world says is good—what the world says is acceptable and normal—God's Word never changes. What was wrong 100 years ago is still wrong today; what was sin 20 years ago is still sin today. I was never one who craved attention or wanted to be in the limelight. I actually preferred to be behind the scenes, but for whatever reason, I was rarely out of public view. I did however, want to be liked and accepted, or so I thought! But how can we desire to be a part of anything that does not put Christ first. The word says, "Love not the world, neither the things that are in the world." (1 John 2:15). Instead of being accepted, should we strive to be set apart—different?

Sometimes we may not love the things in the world, but we don't stand up and voice our repulsion of those things. Silence sometimes means approval. Today, we call it peer pressure. But for me, it wasn't really peer pressure. I don't believe that any of my friends or associates would have treated me differently if I would have stood up for righteousness. I didn't, and I could have. I didn't stand up for a lot of things.

One particular incident occurred in Spanish class that still saddens me today. The teacher left the class, and one of the boys, who was the class clown, told everyone to slide their chairs to the back of the room, far away from the teacher. The plan was to say to this teacher when she returned to class, "A sprinkle a day, helps keep the odor away." When she re-entered the classroom, she looked so shocked. I know she wondered why all of our chairs were at the back of the class. Then all the students began saying the phrase. I started to say it also, until I glanced into her eyes. Her eyes were filled with such humiliation and pain, that I could not continue. Some of the other students looked around and I know they felt the way I did, ashamed. I went back to visit her a couple of years after I graduated from high school, just to say hello. I don't think I ever apologized to her personally, but somehow, I believe she knew how truly sorry I was.

That could have ended very differently for me. I could have walked right into another box—a box of shame—if I had carried out the prank. Yes, I, although I could have repented, and I'm sure I would have done so immediately, chose to resist conforming. But what I did not do was speak up and tell the other students that it was cruel and not to do it. The fact that I moved my chair to the back of the room was an example of loving the world---going along with what I knew to be wrong. There are so many examples of crossroads, where I was presented with choosing right from wrong. I'm sure you have also come to those forks in the road, or done or said things in your youth that you're not proud of. How wonderful it is that God gives us a way of escape.

> **There hath no temptation taken you but such as is common to man: but God is faithful, who will not suffer you to be tempted above that ye are able; but will with the temptation also make a way to escape, that ye may be able to bear it. (I Corinthians 10:13).**

As a teenager, I felt a sense of longing for things that I knew weren't important or good for me. My hair had to be perfect every time I went out of my house. I mean every strand of hair. My makeup had to be perfect. The clothes I wore had to be designer brands. When there was a dance at school, I had to go. If a fellow student gave a party, I had to be there. My mom said that I had a partying spirit. I don't know if that was the case or not, but I felt drawn to the things of the world, when I knew that those things were not the rewarding things of life, but I continued pursuing them despite my inner convictions. I'm not saying that we shouldn't want to look presentable or go to social outings, but we have to examine "the why." For me, these behaviors were the first hints of low self-confidence and social anxiety.

That feeling of low self-confidence grew—that quiet ache of believing I wasn't worth fighting for. It was my sophomore year in high school, and I had qualified for the city track meet in the 100 yd. dash, the 220 yd. dash, and the 440-yard relay. Our track coach scheduled a mandatory practice two days before the meet. Unfortunately for me, the drill team tryouts were the same day and at the same time. I wanted to do both, and instead of discussing it with my parents and my coach, I discussed it with my friends. The details have faded from my memory, but for whatever reason, I understood that my track coach had excused me from practice to attend the drill team tryouts. Instead of confirming with my coach or seeking advice from my parents, I went to the tryouts and skipped track practice.

To my surprise, when I showed up for track practice the following day, my coach informed me that I, along with another teammate, were disqualified from participating in the city-wide track meet because we missed the mandatory track practice. I was so disappointed and hurt. If it had only been the city-wide meet, it may not have had such a detrimental effect on me. However, the city-wide track meet served as a precursor to the district, regional, and ultimately the state championships. Not to mention, that year, I was on track to stand on the podium at the state championships in the 100 and 220 yd. dashes.

I went home crying to my parents, and naturally, my dad and I returned to school to discuss this matter with the coach and principal.

The principal, of course, supported the coach. I explained to the principal that I strongly believed I had been excused from the practice, and did not dismiss track practice as being unimportant. At the meeting, the coach said that she had had announced that we could go to the tryouts, but we either had to have a short practice before the tryouts or a short practice afterwards. I don't recall what was said, but I do know that if I had taken initiative and went to my coach directly before deciding to miss practice, I would not have been put in that predicament.

Although it was my fault, I wanted my dad to fight a little harder for me, explain how not running could affect my future scholarship offers, explain that I hadn't skipped practice out of rebellion—stand up for me. But that wasn't my dad. He was a gentle, kind, loving man, and although he hurt for me, he told me that it was a lesson for me to learn. I didn't see it then, and I still don't think the consequences were fair—considering. As a grandparent now, I think about that day and consistently remind my adult children to ask questions—find out what their kids are doing—make sure their children are making sound decisions because although they think they're grown, they're not. It was a lesson I had to learn the hard way. My parents felt bad for me because they knew how much running in the meet meant to me, but I had to take responsibility for my actions. At least I made the drill team! Decisions come with consequences, regardless of how we come to those decisions.

During the following season, I suffered a serious pulled hamstring which affected my track performance my Senior year. I still qualified for the city and eventually to the state meet, but the pulled muscle did have an effect on my overall mental state—affecting my performance.

In addition to the pulled muscle, my life choices also affected my track career. I loved the sport, but looking back on it now, I could have devoted more time and effort into it, and eliminated the late parties and everything that accompanies that scene. But the grace of the Almighty God was still sufficient! You may be asking, what was the box? It was fear. I thought I knew what I wanted, and I thought certain people in my life were friends, and I wanted to believe that they were. I know now that many of them were not. The word *friendship* is quoted so often without true meaning. Once I realized that the things that I thought were so important and I couldn't live without, were so insignificant when I compared them to the greater plan that God had for my life. It seemed that again I was in a box—peer pressure. The box I entered was one that I thought I could jump into with the intention of jumping right back out. But sometimes, after we jump in, we're stuck, or we are drawn deeper in.

And as far as just being me, sometimes it was challenging for me. There were times when I worried about what other people were going to say or what they would think about me. I remember when I had to wear Gloria Vanderbilt jeans, Giorgio perfume and Puma track shoes. I remember the first time I had a drink. I remember it so well because my mom had told my brother and I that we should avoid alcohol because we had a predisposition to alcoholism due to genetics, heredity and spiritual curses that had been passed down and never broken.

It was lunch time and I had gone to McDonald's with a few friends. The friend who was driving stopped at a store on our way back to school and purchased a forty-ounce bottle of beer. Her older siblings had been drinking for a few years now, so she was very comfortable with it. We parked the car on the street and she took a sip and passed it to one of the other girls in the car, then a third girl, and then finally to me. I was thinking to myself, what have I gotten myself into? Everything that I was taught about right and wrong rushed through my mind, but instead of standing up for righteousness, I walked right into a box. I took my first drink. And how did Satan get me? He got me because I liked the way it made me feel. I had always been so shy and quiet and was unable to talk openly to people, and this is what I wanted. The alcohol gave me a confidence that I did not have otherwise—deception. And the enemy knew what was attractive to me, and he knew that once I walked into that box, it would be difficult for me to get out. That was my senior year.

From that point on, every weekend when my friends and I went to a party, we had a couple of wine coolers or a forty ounce before we stepped into the party. I remember one particular night; I went to a block party up on The Ohio State University campus. It was the night before a big track meet, so I hadn't planned on staying very late. I had been drinking, and I ran into two of my teammates who ran on a relay with me. They walked up to me and gave me a look of total disgust. They knew I had been drinking, and they were so disappointed in me. I can't remember ever having felt so ashamed until that point in my life. I not only was ruining my life, but I was affecting the lives of other people around me. You see we had college scouts looking at us all the time because we had one of the best relays in the city. We ran well, and they forgave me, but I had a hard time forgiving myself. Ephesians 4:32 says, "And be ye kind one to another, tenderhearted, forgiving one another, even as God for Christ's sake hath forgiven you." Again, decisions come with consequences. For me, it goes far beyond drinking the night before a track meet, before a party, or to escape from a painful memory, that first decision to take a drink, lead to years of consequences, embarrassments, strongholds, broken promises and unforgiveness.

17 THE SHATTERED GLASS

High school was some of the best days of my life. Between drill team, track, ensemble, powder puff football, basketball and football games, and school dances, what could be better? I had two boyfriends in high school. One, in 9th grade and tenth, and the other, my junior year in high school, and part of my senior year. I met my first boyfriend at track practice when I ran for a summer track program where my dad was the coach, The Columbus Trailblazers. My dad was so committed to the kids in the club that he went out and purchased a station wagon so he could pick kids up, take them to practice, drive them home and drive them to Saturday track meets during the summer. My mom was so angry with him when he bought at station wagon. He came home one day, pulled up in the driveway, and there it was.

In ninth grade, I was a living witness for Jesus. I introduced my first boyfriend to Christ and talked for hours on the phone about the bible—leading to him getting baptized. He ended up breaking up with me because he was jealous of my best friend, who happened to be a boy. He was convinced that we were more than just friends. I found out years later that he was the one cheating on me with my so-called best girlfriend. God had protected me back then, I didn't even know it.

I met my second boyfriend at this teen dance club. One day, as a group of friends and I were driving to the club, a car pulled up beside us and a group of boys were hanging out of the window with their music blasting. I noticed a boy smiling at me. When we arrived at the club, a carload of boys pulled up shortly after us. The boy who smiled at me sparked up a conversation and that was the start of our relationship. He was a football player and had hopes of going to the NFL. He spent long hours in the gym training in preparation for the transition to collegiate athletics, although he was a year younger than I and had two years before committing to college. However, I understood as I had similar aspirations with track.

As prom season approached, he made excuses as to why he didn't want to go to my prom. All I knew was, it my senior year, had no date and no prospects. No one else asked me and I assumed it was because they presumed, I already had a date. A few weeks before prom, I reached out to my old boyfriend and asked if he would like to go with me as friends. He arrived tipsy and over an hour late, and insisted that we stop by his prom first since it was on the same night. Reluctantly I agreed. When we finally arrived at my prom, it was almost over. I remember walking in, looking around at the picked over food, dispersed crowd—as most people had already left and asked myself, "How did I get here?"

After we left the prom, he drove me to an after-party, left claiming he was making a quick run and coming back. I connected with a few friends, enjoyed the remainder of the night and made a decision to never speak to him again.

My dad and I contacted several colleges and asked their track and field coaches or recruiters to come to a few of my AAU track meets, the summer before entering my senior year. My AAU track coach contacted schools for me as well. Many of them showed up, and several colleges were very interested in my attending their school. By the time track season came around my senior year, I had already received several scholarship offers, and narrowed my list down to my top three.

That Summer after graduating from high school was the most trying Summer of my life up to that point. It was a time for me to let go of friendships and relationships that were holding me back or pushing me in directions that the Lord did not want me to go. Realizing that certain friendships were not in my best interest to hold on to took some time and some help from God. I had two very special friends during my senior year—or so I thought—my best girlfriend and our mutual male friend. He was not, and had not been more than a friend to either of us.

The three of us did everything together! We took the same classes, went to parties, the mall, the sporting events; you name it, we did it together. It started off great but ended in chaos. I thought we would be friends forever, but both friendships ended, leaving me feeling betrayed and used. My girlfriend traveled most of the Summer after graduation and when she returned, shortly after, she left for college and I tried to keep in contact with her—not knowing that I was someone in her past that she wanted to keep in her past. One day, I arranged to go visit her on campus. She knew I was coming and seemed excited over the phone. However, when I arrived at her dorm, she left me there for several hours—attending to things far more important than I.

When I got home, I realized that she had moved on and I didn't hear from her until years later—after I was married and visiting my parents at my childhood home. She stopped by—barely recognizing her—I reminded my mom who she was. We sat and talked for about an hour—reminiscing about old times, and I never heard from her again.

A few weeks before, a few graduating seniors decided to get together to say goodbye, before we all went our separate ways for college. My two best friends—the ones I mentioned previously had planned to be there as well. When I arrived at another mutual friend's house, on one else was there yet. The house was quiet—no laughter, no music. The host told me that others were on their way, so I followed him downstairs to wait. He leaned in and kissed me. At first, I didn't think much of it—just a harmless moment between friends. Things progressed and I told him to stop. I said I didn't want to do anything. He didn't listen. I remember the confusion—the disbelief that someone I knew could ignore my words. I pushed him away, heart racing, and ran upstairs. As I reached the door, my male friend—my best friend—was walking in. He noticed my face, the way I avoided his eyes.

"What's wrong?" he asked.

"Go ask your friend," I said quietly before leaving.

What happened that night didn't just end in that basement—it followed me for years. I thought leaving the house would be the hardest part, but it wasn't. It was what came after. The friend who saw me leaving, the one who asked what was wrong, didn't believe me. He said I made it up because I was embarrassed. He spread rumors—cruel ones—that twisted what happened into something I couldn't recognize. For weeks, he called our house at all hours—hanging up before anyone could answer. He told lies to families in our neighborhood, even to the parents of the children I babysat. The late phone calls got so bad that my mom filed a police report to see if that would keep the phone calls from harassing us during the middle of the night.

Unfortunately, the policed said that there was little or nothing they could do because we didn't have any proof that the boy in question was really the one making the phone calls. She also inquired about getting the phone tapped and a restraining order, but because there had not been any physical threat to me, they were unable to assist us with that either. As far as the rumors were concerned, we contacted an attorney and discussed if we had a case of defamation of character. He told us that we could, but he discouraged it, as it would have been costly, lengthy and would likely cause me more emotional distress.

How could the person I considered my best friend—the only who dropped pizza off at my house late at night when I was hungry—the one who came to all my track meets, gathered my running shoes and sweats from the starting line to the finish line, become the one who haunted my family and me?

I even found out later, after being offered a track scholarship to one school, that the coach had changed her mind because she was informed by someone that I was pregnant and would not be running track that Autumn. Of course, that was a lie invented by my adversary in an attempt to destroy me. Satan went through a lot to try to ruin my future, but God had a greater plan for my life. Even though I had turned my back on Him, he never turned His back on me.

What hurt most wasn't the night itself—it was how quickly people chose to believe the worst instead of the truth. That's the kind of pain that lingers, shaping how you see people, how you love, and how you trust. I can't say for certain who believed the rumors or not—no one asked me. But one thing I do know is that standing up for me something I did not see. Thank God that I had a friend who sticks closer than a brother. (Proverbs 18:24).

I didn't tell anyone what really happened that night in the basement until weeks later, when I finally confided in my brother. I made him promise not to tell, and he didn't. By then, the damage was already done—rumours had spread, and trust felt like something I'd never have again. Confiding in my brother about what had really happened that night–saying it out loud felt like tearing open a wound I'd been pretending didn't exist. My brother just sat there, silent, his face tightening with every word. He didn't ask questions—he didn't have to.

Days before my leaving home to move into the dorms, I spent the evening with a friend. He told me he had heard one side of the story and wanted to know if I was okay. I hadn't expected him to bring it up so I became very emotional and asked him to take me home. As I walked in front door, my mother was sitting on the couch in the front room, as she often was when I went out. Again, she recognized that something was wrong. I told her that I didn't want to talk about it. My brother entered the room and the look on his face gave it away—my mom knew he knew something.

With hesitation, I explained what had happened. When my dad overheard, his reaction was immediate and explosive. I had never seen that kind of fury in his eyes before. My dad was the gentlest soul I knew—always so calm, patient, and compassionate. He went straight to his bedroom, opened a box in his closet and pulled out his gun. He said he was going to the boy's house. My brother jumped up, blocking the doorway, pleading with him to stop. It took everything in his strength to hold him back. My mom was crying and praying, begging him not to go—warning that it would only make matters worse. She was afraid he'd run into the boy's father and that it would turn into something none of us could take back. Through my own tears, I told him there was no point—he had already left for college and I was okay. But my dad kept pacing, jaw tight, hands shaking. I could see the war inside him— the need to protect me, battling against the fear of losing everything if he acted on that anger.

My parents and I visited major universities out of state, small colleges in and out of state and colleges in my home town. I, like most of my friends wanted to go out of State. Especially after all the recent drama, I really wanted to get away, and I felt I needed to get away and have a fresh start. I received several offers for partial scholarships that involved some type of work study program which would have demanded a lot of time and discipline on my part, and honestly, I don't know if I would have been equipped to handle it at that point in my life. I was given a better offer. I was offered a full scholarship to The Ohio State University. You would think I would have been thrilled and thanking and praising God, but I wasn't. I didn't want to stay in my hometown; I wanted to get as far away as I could from everyone in my past. But isn't it good that God knows best, and no matter what we want sometimes, His wants and desires for our life outrank our own? My parents made the decision for me, and I grudgingly accepted the scholarship to Ohio State.

To this day, I'm not sure that I made the right decision by accepting the scholarship, but I have to believe that my steps were ordered by God. Even though my experiences at OSU were not the best, I don't know what my life would have been like if I had gone somewhere else to school. At Ohio State, I met my best friend who is still my best friend today and more like a sister to me. Sometimes we look at our situations, and we think that the grass is greener on the other side. Well, if I would have done this, or if I could have gone there, things would have been different. But we really don't know what the outcome would have been. As a child of God, we have to trust and believe that whatever happens in our life is ultimately good for us. "And we know that all things work together for good to them that love God, to them who are the called according to his purpose" (Romans 8:28).

The day my parents drove me to campus and left me in the dormitory was one of the most overwhelming and frightening days of my life. I was less than 20 miles from my home, but it felt like I was a thousand miles away—far from safety of the expected. I wanted to be independent, but at the same time, I wanted to hold on to what was familiar. I remember standing at the window and watching my parents drive away. It was just me; for the first time in my life, it was just me. That evening when I lay in my dorm room alone, I remember talking to God and asking Him to calm my fears and anxiety and to guide me one day at a time. I knew I was in another box—the unknown. I felt unable to reach out to anyone and form any new friendships. Who could I trust? Would they hurt me as well? Would they accept me—the real me? And to add to my feelings of loneliness and fear, was my misconception of what college was really about.

A week hadn't gone by when I received a call from the boy from the night of the going away get-together. I learned later that he had asked a mutual friend who attended the same college he went to for my number. His voice was shaking. He apologized and asked for my forgiveness. I told him I forgave him, and I meant it. Forgiveness is a choice; it is a decision. Forgiveness does not require reconciliation;

forgiveness does not erase a memory, but it does free yourself from the emotional grip of a painful past.

During my freshman year, I met a nice young man and we began instant friends. We have a few classes together: chemistry and political science. At the time he was heavy into Malcolm X, a charismatic leader who championed Black nationalism and Black pride. As a Christian, I had always viewed him differently, being a Muslim and rejecting Christianity. Although through my friendship, I learned that Malcolm X's beliefs moved far beyond religious beliefs—advocating Black people to defend themselves against white violence, while also urging the Black community to be self-sufficient, support Black-owned businesses, and take political power in their own communities. These concepts were foreign to me, yet reminded me of my experience in fourth grade when my Blackness—rooted in a belief of racial superiority, left me feeling inadequate—not good enough.

We often studied together—specifically Chemistry—testing theories. One afternoon, he shared with me that his roommate had warned him about "girls like me." He told him that I would never be interested in him, and that I was only using him to get a good grade. I'm not sure why he told me; I didn't know what his roommate meant by "girls like me", but it hit hard. First, I considered him a friend—not a boyfriend. Eventually, our friendships drifted apart, and I can only presume his roommates' words made him question my motives.

A few years after I graduated from college, I heard that his roommate had been killed in an automobile accident. The news stunned me—not because I had ever wished anything bad on him, but because it stirred a memory, I thought I had long forgotten. I remembered the words he had spoken against me, words that once left me wounded and confused.

And in that moment, a scripture rose quietly in my heart, "Touch not My anointed, and do My prophet no harm" (Psalm 105:15). Not as a declaration of punishment, but as a reminder that God sees what we endure long before justice, healing, or understanding ever catch up to our stories. It made me reflect on how God shields His children—even when we don't recognize it at the time—and how He handles what we were never meant to carry.

The first major shock was that I really had to study. The second was that I had to wake up on my own, and do it early enough to get breakfast. The breakfast thing wasn't so bad, but when I received my first quarter grades, that took me for a loop. I went from being a straight "A" student to a "C" student. I couldn't believe it; I never had to actually read and study all the material before. My grades did improve, but never to the level that I wanted them to. It seems as though I was just going through the motions. I was going to class most of the time and trying to study, but I lacked motivation. Resentment had me bound, and then add depression and loneliness to that. Sometimes parents have to make decisions that they honestly feel is best, and there's no manual that tells you what to do and what not to do, so you go with your gut. But when you're a child, a teenager, or even an adolescent, you don't understand that. Now that I'm an adult, a wife, and a mother, I tell my children the same thing. "This is the decision that I'm making. "Every decision might not be the best one, but you do what you think is best. That lesson wasn't easy, and I didn't learn it overnight. Actually, it took a lifetime!

OUT OF THE BOX

During college, I went through frightening periods of my life. I remember taking this class on the origins of religion. I, being a Christian, thought this would be an excellent opportunity for me to learn about the history of Christianity, but something quite the contrary happened. We studied Buddhism, Confucianism, Taoism, Hinduism, and others. I really thought I knew enough about the Word of God and had a close enough relationship with the Lord to be able to stand strong and not doubt. To my surprise, when I began to study these other religions, and found that they had similar beliefs as Christianity, I began to wonder. How do we know that what we believe is right? I never doubted the existence of God or the deity of Christ, but I did wonder if perhaps the same God that I served was the same God that those other religions believed in too, but He related to them in a different way.

I remember reading this one particular story about a flood, in which the earth was destroyed by water, and according to our professor, the text we read it from, was dated earlier than the flood in Noah's time. Little did I know that these false religions toy with young people's minds and people who have never had a relationship with the Lord, and are very persuasive. Satan has a tactic that is so smooth that he convinces young people, especially those who are out there searching for answers to life's biggest questions, that the Bible is merely filled with short stories and fables, and not the truth written by men who were divinely inspired by God. I am so thankful that the Word of God was instilled me as a child. Otherwise, I possibly would have been deceived into accepting the lies of the enemy.

Shortly after the quarter had ended, and the class was over, I really began to search God's word for myself and tried to develop a closer relationship with him. I did not ever want to question what I believed again. I wanted to know that I *knew* what I always thought I knew. While I stayed on campus, my roommate and I started meeting with *The Fellowship of Christian Athletes* and *Campus Crusade for Christ*. These two groups truly helped me to stay in tune with what I believed. While striving to develop my relationship with the Lord, I was exploring my thoughts, feelings, emotions, and philosophies. At the same time, I was also being tried in my track career. Going from high school competition to collegiate competition was also a shock back into reality. The great athletes in high school in one city, eventually all meet up together with the other great athletes in another. When that happens, the great ones aren't so great anymore; they're all the same. The phenomenal few, now, they are the ones who are *great!*

I had become average; as did most of my teammates. Our team did have one *great* runner, and I was given the opportunity to run on relays with her. That was very exciting. Even still, I felt that I could have also been *great* if I had made better choices earlier on, and during my years at OSU. The athletic demands in college were so different! We practiced practically all year long. We practiced twice a day beginning in the early Spring, and again in early Autumn, and traveled almost every weekend during the Autumn, Winter, and Spring. My teammates and I trained together, ate together, studied together, roomed together, and traveled together. The experience was more than I had bargained for.

While preparing for my first collegiate meet, my coach announced what events each runner was participating in, and when she got to my name, she stated that I would be running the 400-meter dash and the 4 x 400-meter relay. My heart felt like it had fallen from my chest cavity to my stomach, and my stomach turned like I had just finished drinking a glass of sour milk. I couldn't believe it! Although I had run the 1600-meter relay in high school, I had never run the 400 meters in my life! I was not recruited to run that event! A fear came over me like never before. Yes, I was afraid to run this event, but most importantly, I did not want to run it. As a matter of fact, I hated running it. And it seemed from that point on, my track career went deeper and deeper down the drain.

It didn't have to go down the tube, but it did, only because I allowed it to. I wanted so desperately to tell my coach that I didn't feel comfortable running this event and that I would rather run an event that I was used to, being that it was my first collegiate meet. But I said nothing. At first, I thought that maybe she was just trying some new things out and trying to explore other avenues with the new team, so I waited. The season went on, and week after week after week, I was put in the same events and performed terribly in them. I suppose I thought my coach would realize that she had made a wrong choice in placing me those events and would switch me to different events, but she never did, and I never spoke up! It was a wrong choice; it was a bad choice. I chose to place myself in a box, and I chose to stay there.

I wanted to climb out, or better yet I wanted someone else to let me out. I wanted to talk to my dad about it because he coached me for several years when I was younger, but I felt that I was an adult now and that I had to handle it myself. I rehearsed in my mind what I would say to my coach, over and over again, but I couldn't let the words out. I felt that if I would only be given an opportunity to train for and run the 200-meter dash, that I could have performed excellent in this event. I saw how the sprinters were trained for this event in college and I compared it to the way I had been trained and taught to run this event in high school and earlier on, and I knew that with the proper training I could have run it well. Unfortunately for me, I didn't speak up, and at the beginning of my junior year, I gave up, and I never found out how I could have done.

That Autumn, my coach contacted me and gave me the date, time, and location of the team's annual medical examination, and I did not show up. What I had loved had become something that I hated with a passion. I knew that quitting the track team would mean giving up my scholarship and moving back home, but it was something that I felt I should have done at the time. Of course, now as I look back on it, I wish I had spoken up to my coach about what events I really felt comfortable in, and what type of training I felt I needed to accomplish my goals. I even considered asking my dad to go with me to discuss this with the coach, but I felt that I was an adult and that those actions were not appropriate for a college student. How would it look bringing daddy in to tell the coach that my baby doesn't want to run the 400 meters or to ask to please let her run the 200 meters? I called my dad and told him that I did not go to the physical exam and that I did not want to run anymore. I told him that it was not fun for me any longer, and that I would suffer what every consequence came with my decision. I seemed to conveniently leave out the fact that I still loved to run and that I wanted an opportunity to try a different event. It was the easy way out for me; no conflicts or confrontations.

My dad contacted the athletic department and informed the coach that I was quitting the team. We paid her a visit, and naturally her concern, and the concern of the other athletic staff was the scholarship. What about the money? There were no questions about me, or my decision to stop running or my personal feelings or troubles, but they wanted to know about the scholarship. I remember looking at one of the athletic counselors and saying, "I don't want the scholarship." She looked as if she had seen a ghost. Again, I said, "You can give the scholarship to someone else; I just want to go home."

And that's exactly what I did; I moved back home. Somehow my parents managed to pay for the remainder of my college and I graduated two years later. Yes, I felt as if I had lost something dear and special to me. I had lost a love of mine and a gift from God because I was unable to face my fear and move past it. But God's love and His grace and mercy were always present with me. Although He was present with me, I stayed trapped in that box. A pattern was beginning to develop. When things got too much for me to handle, instead of sticking with it, I ran! I ran to keep from being hurt again. This type of flight response became my coping mechanism—my method of protecting myself.

Even though I was physically out of one box, the spirit that kept driving me inside of these boxes and keeping me in them, continued to have a hold on me. My personal life during college had taken a giant step backwards since high school. I mostly stayed to myself. My college roommate was, and still is a very important person in my life. She and I went to high school together and were friends, but our friendship didn't really grow until college. My best friend, who I met in college was one of my rivals in track in high school.

It is ironic how God brought us together. They are both very important people in my life today, along with another teammate in high school and college. A guard had been put up. I met a lot of people in college, hung out with other students, but I did not allow myself to let anyone in far enough to risk getting let down again. I lost of part of myself. There were times when I wanted to talk to people and get to know them, but I couldn't risk being let down—betrayed again. I remember sometimes sitting in the student union or even at a block party or union party, and being surrounded my hundreds of people and feeling all alone.

    I did not have that inner peace that comes from knowing the Lord. I knew Him, but I didn't really know Him. Even after moving back home, I still continued to hang out in the bars on campus or at the clubs on the weekend. I wanted a closer relationship with the Lord, but I refused to crucify my flesh. "Jesus said, '...If any man will come after me, let him deny himself, and take up his cross daily, and follow me'" (Luke 9:23). The cycle needed to be broken. The cycle that could only be broken by His power, His love, His everlasting grace.

Betrayal

Dubonna L Dawkins

Feeling deceived
Yet not knowing if it was deception
Or truth

Wanting to believe so badly that the words spoken were
From the heart
Being unsure and hurting deep within
Due to uncertainty

Still longing for what you know to be death
To your soul
Death to your body
Separation from all that is good

Not knowing how to let go

Not wanting to let go

While wanting to let go

Wishing to be a fly on the wall
Maybe on a wall where secrets are
Revealed

Perhaps on a wall where intents of the heart are
Bounced off
Listening to the voices
Behind the door

Remembering the Words you read in
The Holy Book
Reminiscing on mother's words
Father's words

To know if it was real in the realm of now is

Meaningless

Nevertheless…needing to know

18 GROWING INTO HER

I started working for the Columbus Recreation and Parks Department part-time during the Summer after my Junior year and during the school year my Senior year. I met my husband during my Senior year. We worked at the same recreation center. Dating my husband was different than anything I had experienced before. Although I had dated before, those relationships were with boys, not men, figuring it out themselves, just like I was. My husband, ten years my senior, carried himself differently. His actions reflected a steadiness, a maturity, and a sense of responsibility that stood out immediately. He took my car to get washed and filled up my gas tank weekly. He sat down and had full conversations with my dad, attended church every Sunday and prayed with and for me.

Shortly after graduation from college, we got married. He, like myself, were just beginning to desire a true intimate relationship with the Lord. We began reading the Word together and growing closer to the Lord, but I still felt an emptiness inside that I really could not explain. Have you ever been in a church service and it seems that everyone else around you are feeling the power of God, but you felt nothing? Well, this happened to me practically every Sunday. I went away from the service saying, "Lord, there has to be more." I thought that maybe there was something wrong with me or perhaps I had done something that the Lord had not forgiven me of—I didn't know. For a while I just stopped going to church as much. I would go, maybe once a month, twice tops, while my husband was still going every Sunday. He began going to Sunday School, and some Sundays after Sunday school was over, he would drive back home and pick me up for Church. This went on for about a year until I became pregnant with our first daughter.

During this time, I was working in retail management. My boss was an atheist who grew up in a home where there was no mention of God. She was married to a Jew who had rejected Judaism in his adulthood. We didn't discuss spirituality much; she knew I went to church, but she never quite understood why. She would ask me, "So you really believe this stuff?" I told her that I had grown up in the church and had believed all of my life. To not believe in God and Jesus was something that I could never imagine. Despite our differences, we got along very well. We became very close. My best friend from college also got married and moved to Texas and I had very few other friends. Well anyway, my boss and I started going out to lunch together and shopping and what not, and I honestly thought we had a pretty good friendship. She even nominated me for Assistant Manager of the Year for our entire region and gave me an excellent recommendation.

I was blessed to win the award, and because of it, I was the next candidate for the new store that the company was planning to open in a new mall that was being developed downtown. I was excited and saw a lucrative future with this company. Not more than a few months after this, my boss told me that she and her husband were planning a vacation to California to visit his parents. You see, they were both originally from California. She had visited California about a year before when I was first hired on. I felt very comfortable and confident in my ability to handle the operations of the store while she was out of town. My regional manager called me and informed me that if I needed anything while my boss was out of town to give her a call.

I remember closing up this one particular evening. I, along with two other girls were working the evening shift. Like always, close to closing, I began closing the register and counting the money and completing the deposit slip for the Monday morning. This was a Saturday night, and I wouldn't be able to make a deposit until Monday. I put the deposit in the safe as normal, without locking it, and exited the store and locked the gate as always. You notice I said without locking the safe. We had a problem with the safe. Since my first day on the job, the safe had a default in it and we were unable to lock in and open it without a lot of difficulty. Because of this, my manager just told me and the head cashier not to lock it and for almost two years we did not lock it.

I don't know why the manager never requested to have the safe fixed or replaced. To my knowledge, she never mentioned to the regional manager. Actually, when the regional manager came in to town, which was only maybe once every three or four months, she would lock the safe, but it took her a long time to get it unlocked again. Anyway, the next morning when I went to work, I didn't look in the safe because we had enough money in the register from the previous night and it was a Sunday morning as I stated earlier, and the bank was not open.

At the end of the business day on Sunday, I closed the store down as usual and counted the drawer and began completing another deposit slip when I noticed that the deposit from Saturday evening was missing. Talk about freaking out. I couldn't believe it. I looked everywhere; behind the counter on the floor. When I finally concluded that it was nowhere to be found, I called my regional manager at her office and of course, her answering machine came on.

I remembered that she had left her home telephone number for me in case of emergency so I called her home. Her husband answered the phone, and I told him who I was and that it was an emergency and that I needed to speak with her. But she was not home, so I asked him to please have her call me when she got in. I even went so far as to leave him my home telephone number. I did not however, tell him the specifics of the emergency. And of course, she did not return my call. I drove home, with a very sick feeling on my stomach. I did not know what to do. I could not sleep that night. My husband tried to get me to relax and not worry about it, but it was no use, I couldn't get it off of my mind. I relieved the entire episode over and over again in my mind. I even began doubting whether I had put the money in the safe, but I know I did. I reported for work on Monday and I called the regional manager's office again. This time I reached her. I explained everything to her and she asked me why I did not call her. I told her that I had left a message with her husband, but she did not respond. I still don't know to this day whether her husband told her I had called or not. The regional manager told me that she would be in town during the week to investigate the matter. My boss returned the following day, Tuesday, or so she said.

When my boss showed up for work, I told her that the deposit was missing. We discussed it, and she told me not to worry about it, but I couldn't help it. The regional came in to town on Wednesday, she didn't waste any time. She and the manager went in to the back room and talked for a while and I worked the front counter. She then asked me to come back and speak with her. She asked me again to explain what had happened. I told her. She asked why I had not locked the safe. I told her that we never locked the safe by order of the manager, but the manager denied it. It was then that I knew I was dealing with a snake.

She completely turned her back on me. She had the nerve to tell me, I told you guys that if anyone asked anything about the safe being kept unlock, I would deny it. You're going down alone. The regional then asked me for my resignation. I told her that I was not going to resign, and if she wanted me to leave, she was going to have to fire me. She said, "Alright then, you are fired." I then told her that she was going to have to fire me in front of a witness. She asked me several times to leave the store, but I refused. I told her I wasn't leaving until I had a witness that would testify for me that she fired me. She then said that she was going to call security. I told her to call them; I wanted her to call them.

A few minutes passed, and the security officer entered the store. He asked the manager what the problem was. She told him that I refused to leave. He asked me why I wouldn't leave, and I explained that I had just been fired, and I wanted her to fire me in front of a witness, and I wasn't walking out until she did. The security officer asked the manager if she had fired me and she said told him that I had been fired. I then asked the security office if he heard her say I was fired and he said, "Yes, he had heard her." I then asked him if I needed him to testify as to the fact that I was hired, if he would. He told me that he would. Then I told him, "Okay, now I'm leaving."

I was so strong. That is until I got in the mall, and then I broke down and started crying. I went to a pay phone and called my husband and told him that I had been fired and for him to pick me up. He showed up a few minutes later, and we went home. I remember leaving the mall and looking back at that store and thinking to myself, you're going to close your doors. I didn't pray this or ask God to bring any harm to the store, but somehow, I knew that that business wasn't going to last, well at least not in that particular location. And don't you know, about two years later that store went out of business. Now I'm not saying that my being fired unjustly was the cause of the store going out of business, but somehow, I just knew.

Now looking back on the entire period, the Lord was merely protecting me. He pulled me out of a potentially harmful friendship. Even though my injustice, if truth be told, hurt me dramatically, the hurt I felt momentarily was far better than the risk of my being persuaded away from my relationship with the Lord. I don't believe I would have been swayed, but God is all knowing. And I do know that all things work together for the good of those who love the Lord and are the called, according to His purpose. Now, remember that not all things are good that happen to believers, but the Lord will take all of those not so good things and still make them work together so that the end result is all good.

OUT OF THE BOX

Break the Cycle

Dubonna L Dawkins

End it
Break the cycle of abuse
Generation after generation falling into tempestuous gales
Weathering the storms instead of fleeing to safety
End it
Break the cycle of poverty
Begin to place value on the life The Creator has given you
Stop limiting your potential and
embracing feelings of unworthiness
End it
Break the cycle of promiscuity
Bring to a close the measure of beauty and self-worth
By how tight the clothes
Cease the sharing of your temple with the gutter
Giving into dogs who are not capable of showing you love
Allowing them to beat your body
disrespect your mind, murder your Spirit
End it
Break the cycle of enslavement
Filling your mind with notions of contempt
Using you for their own gratification
Not giving in to marriage; not giving your children a name
Leaving you with nothing but shame
Robbing you of your identity
Draining your strength
Depositing seeds of guilt and condemnation
Break the cycle

19 MY JOURNEY TO THE UPPER ROOM

Not even a year after I was released from that position, I became pregnant with my first daughter. It was during that time when I started studying about the Baptism with the Holy Spirit. I read a lot about it and I talked with my mother about it, but I didn't fully understand it. I had visited a Pentecostal church that a friend of mine attended. That was a frightening experience for me. During the service, people started talking in these different languages all around me. I had no idea what was going on; you see nothing like this ever happened at my church.

Later that evening when my mom and I got home, I had so many questions that I needed answered. She tried to explain to me that that was the way the Pentecostals worshiped and that on the day of Pentecost, when the disciples were in the upper room, and the Holy Ghost fell, they all spoke in other tongues. What a glorious day!

From that point on, I wanted the gift of speaking in tongues, but I did not want something coming in taking over my body and forcing me to speak in a different tongue. You see, I had not been taught that the Holy Spirit is a gentleman, and that speaking in an unknown tongue was an act of faith. I had been baptized with water unto repentance, but I also desired to be baptized with the Holy Ghost, and with fire (Matthew 2:11). Acts 1:8 tells us "But ye shall receive power, after that the Holy Ghost is come upon you." I wanted that power, but I didn't know how to get it. While searching for that power, I was blessed to be able to collect unemployment for my wrongful discharge from my former position.

I was about eight months pregnant when I attended a Wednesday night prayer service at a friend's church. The pastor asked for anyone who was suffering from a demonic stronghold to come forth for prayer. At that time, I was not sure what a demonic stronghold was, but before I knew it, I was down at the altar. The pastor told everyone to lift up their hands and receive deliverance from the Lord. I wasn't sure what was going on, and I wasn't really paying attention to what the pastor was saying. All I know was that all around me, men and women, were speaking in that unknown tongue again, and I wanted to do it too. I remember opening my mouth and simply speaking whatever came out of it. I only spoke a few words, but I continued speaking them over and over and over again. A force did not come over my body and force my lips to speak, but I began speaking words that I had never spoken before, and I just knew it was the gift of tongues. I can't explain to you how I knew; I just did.

I forgot about why I had gone to the alter in the first place. When I opened my eyes, I remember looking up and hearing the pastor telling everyone to take their seats. I hurried back to my seat where my mother and friend were sitting and telling my mom with so much excitement that I had spoken in tongues. My mom told me not to doubt what I had spoken and that when we left the enemy would try to convince me that I was making up words to say. And of course, as soon as we got in the car, those thoughts came in my head, but I immediately cast them down and continued thanking the Lord for giving me this gift. Every day after that my faith got stronger and stronger and my prayer language got better and better. And now I know!

After my unemployment ended, I took another retail management position which I kept up until I was ready to deliver. I decided not to return to work for a while after I had our first child. I stayed home with her for about six months and it was during this period when I received a vision from the Lord to open a Christian daycare center. I had never really had any interest in working in the child care field before, but I did want to be able to work and be a helpmeet for my husband and still be able to spend time with my daughter as well. I had a plan. From there I decided to take a position as a co-teacher in a daycare center. My plan was to be able to earn a little income while being able to spend time with my daughter, as well as, learning as much as I could about the childcare business.

I started working part time in the mornings. My mother-in-law watched my daughter every morning until she turned 18 months, then I began taking her to the daycare with me. This worked out very well. I was blessed to be able to take her with me free of charge. Even though the pay wasn't the greatest, our needs were met. I stayed there until I had my second daughter.

After her birth, I experienced a severe case of postpartum depression. For months after I delivered, I had no clue why I was having the thoughts that I was having, but I knew that it was not normal. I had thoughts of hurting myself and others. I remember walking into my doctor's office and sharing the thoughts that were running throw my mind, feelings of isolation, anxiety, crying episodes and very low energy. He told me that I was experiencing postpartum depression. The relief I felt was huge—knowing that what I was experiencing had a name. He prescribed Prozac. Reluctantly, I began taking it. Like many black families, medication, especially for mental illness is frowned upon. My mom's advice was "Just Pray." Another box had surrounded me. This time it was just life—building a box around me.

Unfortunately for me, praying alone was not enough. I started seeing some improvement in my symptoms after a few weeks, but my family also started noticing changes in my behavior. I remember my husband looking at me one day and saying, "You're just too nice! That medicine is making you too nice! You're not acting like you!" I remember being agreeable to everything. Nothing affected me. I felt like I was floating on fluffy clouds. After several trial and errors, I found the right medicine and dosage to help me during that period. I share this to encourage someone else that may be experiencing something similar. I believe that the earth is the Lord's and the fullness thereof (Psalm 24:1). In other words, God created the earth and many things found in nature are used for medicine, including plants and herbs. So instead of looking at taking medication as a lack of faith, view it as taking advantage of God's creation. During this time, I took another leave of absence and returned to the center when my daughter was about 4 months old. My mother-in-law helped us out again. Thank the Lord for Grandmas!

There was a woman who worked at the daycare who was a professed witch. Another co-worker, who became a great friend, and I, were the only Christians who worked at the daycare. The daycare was planning their annual Halloween party and I had recently learned about the history of Halloween, originating from the Celtic festival that marked the end of summer and the beginning of winter. The Celts believed that on Samhain, the boundary between the living and the dead became blurred, and the spirits of the dead would return to earth. To ward off ghosts, people would light bonfires, wear costumes, and dance around them. I understand that most people today, either don't know the true meaning behind Halloween, or have decided to celebrate it anyway because their reason is just for fun.

Regardless of other's opinions, I had made a decision to not celebrate it and not participate in the party. I asked the director if I would be permitted to leave work early that day. She understood and allowed me to take part of the day off. I remember sitting in circle time with a group of students. This teacher, the professed witch, was also sitting in the circle. I notice her staring at me and my spirit became was uneasy. The Holy Spirit in me was in war with the spirit that was operating in her. I remember yawning and looking over at this teacher and noticed her watching my every move. Instantly, I recognized that she was attempting to cast a spell on me. Some of you reading this may not believe in such things, but I know that spiritual warfare is real. I immediately began praying in the spirit under my breath. It was that day, the Lord gifted me with the spirit of discernment. I had only heard about discernment and didn't understand it fully, but after that day, the Lord began showing me things that in the natural, I would have no knowledge of. I had to learn what to do with the information God was giving me.

I stayed employed at that daycare until I delivered my third daughter. After her birth, I did not return back to the daycare. Instead, I decided to open an in-home childcare center of my own. I learned shortly after I left that daycare, I learned that the teacher, the professed witch, had been killed in a hit and run accident. It was after that incident that I learned that God's vengeance is still alive today, and the power of God had become real to me. I had no doubt of my relationship with God and His love for me.

Again, I'm not suggesting by any means that we should wish ill upon anyone. But what I do know is that God shows up, time and time again, that He is a faithful God, and He is not a man that He should lie. (Numbers 23:19) According to **Romans 12:17-19, the scripture tells us to not repay evil for evil and to have regard for good things in the sight of all men. We are commanded to live in peace with all men and not avenge ourselves, but to give no place for wrath, for it is written, "Vengeance is Mine" says the Lord. It is a promise to those who come into covenant with God.

Empower Me

Dubonna L Dawkins

I will look within my being
I will uncover my gifts and talents
I will allow myself to want to succeed
I will work towards making my dreams a reality

I will believe in myself
I will work to better my life
I will uncover my weaknesses and shortcomings
I will allow myself to grow
I will work with regard to being a better person

I will love myself
I will forgive myself
I will learn from my mistakes
I will accept people for who they are
I will listen to those who love me
I will learn from the errors of others
I will trust myself
I will not doubt

I will empower me

20 THE TEST

I had received the Baptism of the Holy Ghost, excited about my next opportunity and full of hope. I went through the process of getting licensed to operate a childcare center, which included going back to college for some additional courses. I ran this in-home childcare business for nearly two years and I learned a tremendous amount in the field. I knew that God had something greater, just waiting around the corner. I felt that the vision the Lord had given me years earlier, was about to come to pass. The steps of a man (or woman) are ordered by the Lord (Psalm 37:23). God already had it worked out!

At first, my father and I researched starting our own in-home child care center. My dad—ever supportive—renovated the basement of our childhood home so I could start one there. I remember watching him work—each nail, each brushstroke filled with the promise of something beautiful. But after all that effort and anticipation, the fire department couldn't approve the space. There was no direct exit to the outside. Just like that, my dream hit a wall. I was heartbroken, but not ready to let go. I knew however, that the Lord had given me a vision of a Christian daycare center. That is when the Lord told me to take my vision to the Pastor of my church and present it to him. The idea was grasped immediately. Actually, the Pastor had had a similar vision, and he shared, my coming forth was a confirmation. For the next two years, I began my preparation for the vision God had given me. I knew that my Pastor would have to take it before the Trustees of the church and the church body, but I wanted to be ready. I knew that it was only a matter of time, and it was all on God's time anyway.

I continued running my in-home day care and took some additional college courses to better prepare me for the center I knew I would one day operate. My pastor and I discussed board members for the day care and presented our proposal to the church body at the church board meeting. The church voted in favour of the day care. We were on our way. The entire process, after the church approved the day care, took about one year. The church had already built onto the existing church structure for additional Sunday school classes, and as it turned out, the daycare was given those classrooms to share.

My next step was to form a board of directors. I invited someone who had been a longtime friend of my husband—someone I believed was wise, dependable, and capable of leadership. At the time, I was certain I had made the right choice. Before finalizing everything, I spoke with my pastor about having my husband serve on the board. I worried it might seem like a conflict of interest. To my relief—and maybe a little naively—he said it would be fine, as long as my husband didn't vote on matters involving my salary or benefits. I remember leaving that conversation full of gratitude and anticipation, unaware that what felt like the start of something good would one day carry a different kind of weight.

I had a similar conversation with my husband's friend, and in front of both of us, he seemed to agree that having my husband on the board wouldn't be a problem. He nodded, smiled, and gave every impression of support. But when the board finally met for the first time, and another member voiced concern that my husband shouldn't serve, he sat there in silence. Not a word in my defence. Not even a glance in my direction. In that moment, something in me shifted. The trust I had placed in him wavered, and I realized he was not the man I had believed him to be. For the first time, I questioned his probity—and quietly, I began to question my own judgment too.

I felt that there had been some miscommunication in regards to starting the daycare. I honestly don't believe that anything was done purposely, but it was just a feeling that I had. I wasn't confident that the church was ready to embrace the daycare as a part of its body. I felt separation arise at the onset of the opening of the center. The daycare was started to operate as a ministry of my church, but for legal reasons, the center was formed under a different name as a separate corporation. In the event the daycare was taken to court, the church could not be touched. I began interviewing for my assistant and all was hopeful. I was so excited that the Lord had brought the vision to fruition. Unfortunately, slowly but surely, my excitement and joy began to decline.

We posted the position of Assistant Director within the church. To my surprise, there was very little response to the role from the church body. Going into this ministry, I had envisioned the daycare being filled with church members, as teachers and teacher's aids, but just the opposite occurred. It seems from that point on, I knew I was on my own, so to speak.

There was always the support from the Pastor and my family. Fortunately, I was able to hire one church member to cook and another to serve as the Assistant Director. When I realized I needed to recruit teachers from outside the church, God blessed me with a few wonderful additions to our team. During those first few months, everything I had envisioned the preschool to be came to life. The students were learning about God, their ABCs, Art, Science, and so much more.

But as we continued to grow, the need for additional staff increased—and unfortunately, the harmony we had once enjoyed began to shift into discord. Some staff began to disregard rules, challenge decisions, and avoid accountability. This was difficult for me because my core beliefs have always been to follow the rules, respect authority, and take responsibility for your actions. As a result, I found myself deeply dependent upon many of my family members to keep the learning center open and operating efficiently. If it had not been for those faithful few, the daycare would have gone under within the first few months.

Reflecting back on it now, I recall a post I read on social media a while back. The post read, "Unmet expectations are one of the leading reasons why couples divorce." After reading it, I realized the same principle applies to all relationships—friendships, workplace relationships, and business partnerships. I had expectations that staff would honor the rules, respect decisions even when they disagreed, and remain accountable. But those expectations were not met—and the weight of that reality was hard for me to face.

I came from a close-knit family. Our summers were spent on family vacations, and Sundays meant dinner around the table—fried chicken, collard greens, mashed potatoes, and macaroni and cheese. Though my dad wasn't a regular churchgoer, he was a man of integrity—the kindest man I've ever known. My mom was deeply involved in the church when I was little, a member of the Scholarship Group and Loyal Ladies. I still remember her fancy hats and white gloves. Growing up, a few lessons were ingrained in me: Do unto others as you would have them do unto you; Your word is your bond, and God never changes—His rules are there to protect us. And just as God's laws are meant to guide us, we are also called to respect the laws of the land. My mom often told my brother and me about her father, whom everyone called Papa. She said he never signed contracts or even shook hands on a deal—his word was enough. If he said something, you could count on it. Those values became part of who I was—and that's all I knew. The challenges were not only unfamiliar, but disappointing.

Not only was I disappointed in the actions of some of the staff, but I also felt unsupported by the board. In childcare, the rules and regulations are specific and non-negotiable, especially when it comes to maintaining ratios and ensuring children's safety. For example, children can never be left alone in a classroom without supervision. A teacher cannot work on their own homework when they are responsible for watching children—this is considered theft of time. Teachers also cannot sit on a bench on the playground while children climb and swing, because doing so puts the children at risk. I knew that when these rules were broken, there needed to be consequences.

However, whenever I gave feedback or took corrective action, certain staff members bypassed me and went directly to one board member with their complaints. Instead of directing them back to follow the proper chain of command, their concerns were entertained. This not only undermined my authority but also weakened the structure needed for a safe, accountable, and well-run program.

One incident in particular stands out. I was doing my normal rounds—visiting each classroom and conducting teacher observations. The Assistant Director, who was also assigned to a classroom for half the day, had his laptop open and was making personal phone calls. When I asked what he was working on, he told me he was doing tasks for one of the board members' businesses. I reminded him that he was out of ratio and was not giving his students the attention required. He became agitated and told me he would "take it up with the board member."

That moment deepened my concerns about the lack of respect for me, as well as the lack of separation between the church and the learning center, and the division I had felt from the very beginning grew stronger. Soon after, I started hearing casual comments from church members referring to the center as "that day care" or "the Dawkins' daycare." I would gently correct them by saying, "It's not my daycare; the daycare belongs to the church. I am the Executive Director, but not the owner." Over time, I discovered that many church members genuinely believed the center belonged to me. Three years later, I even learned that one of the board members thought I owned the daycare and was renting space from the church. That misunderstanding explained much of the tension, the misplaced expectations, and the lack of support I had experienced.

I decided that I wasn't going to allow Satan to discourage me and I believed that one day the church would learn to accept the center as its own. Starting off, we made a lot of mistakes. Our first major mistake was that a proper foundation was not laid before we actually opened.

By proper foundation I mean that basic policies and procedures were not put in place before opening. We failed to implement an attendance policy, discipline policy, grievance policy—you name it.

It wasn't that we were lax in coming up with policies; It was simply that we were all new to this business, and we didn't have direct experience. Yes, I went to school and took additional classes in childcare, and I did a lot of research, but some things you just can't get from books. Some things you can't truly understand until you're actually in it. We had everything we needed in accordance with daycare licensing—the equipment, supplies, and forms to operate the learning center, but no experience in the childcare culture.

Childcare is a low paying industry. Most people who enter the field do so because they have a sincere love for children. However, many also believe that it's an easy job—just babysitting. And to the contrary, childcare provides crucial early childhood development for children. High-quality child care helps children develop cognitive, social, and emotional skills, improves school readiness, and can lead to better long-term educational outcomes.

Even more important than policies and procedures, our mistake was assuming that our employees already understood what was expected of them—and how they were to carry out the ministry God had placed them in. There was a lack of unity, a lack of shared vision, and a lack of spiritual awareness that this work was God's work. Because of that, many could not comprehend that the vision before us was something God had called us to steward and bring to pass. Shortly afterwards, my supervisor resigned. She never shared her true reasons for leaving, but I knew the disrespect she had been receiving from the staff had become unbearable. Fortunately, she was offered another role and I wished her the best. Yet, I was still hopeful and determined to see it through.

Then it happened—a full-fledged attack. I notified all the staff and told them that I wanted us to come together and pray for the center and to thank and praise God for blessing us to be able to open our doors and seek His direction. Everyone showed up and it was a blessed evening; the Holy Spirit ruled and reigned that night. We anointed all the classrooms and furnishings, prayed for each other, uplifted and encouraged each other. It was a blessing. It was a Friday; I'll never forget it.

Early Monday morning, I received a phone call from one of the teachers, informing me that my assistant had not showed up to open the building and no one, not even his wife, knew where he was. He just disappeared. He didn't stop by; he didn't call, and he didn't write for weeks. All I knew was that I was left to carry the load of running the center alone, although I knew I wasn't alone—the Lord was with me. The Lord directed me to a scripture in Isaiah that reminded me not to fear because I could trust that He was always with me.

> **Fear thou not; for I am with thee: be not dismayed; for I am thy God: I will strengthen thee; yea, I will help thee; yea, I will uphold thee with the right hand of my righteousness. (Isaiah 41:10).**

And like the pattern I often repeated in my life, I chose to bear this burden alone. We as believers can wallow in self-pity and try to convince ourselves that everybody else has forsaken us and that nobody offers to lend a helping hand, but the Bible clearly states in James 4:2

that we have not because we ask not. Also, in Matthew 11:12 it states that the violent take it by force. Sometimes we tend to believe that everyone else can read our minds or that things should come easily, but people can't and things don't.

To keep things from falling apart, I began working twelve-hour days; I opened the center at 6:00 a.m. and closed it at 6:00 p.m. Why? I don't know. Maybe I felt a sense of obligation and commitment to the center, being that I shared in the vision. Or maybe it was just like I felt when I was a little girl and Victor used to chase me home and threaten to beat me up. I thought I could handle that too. I was strong enough to just take it. Or maybe it was just like when I was in college and my track coach didn't give me an opportunity to run the events, I thought I was best at. I thought I could just handle it. Months went by and I wore myself out.

The Lord did however, send me a few good and faithful people to help me through this trial—a young woman who I quickly promoted to staff supervisor. The Bible gives us a perfect illustration of how God showed a great leader that he did not have to do it all, and to be everything to everybody to be an effective leader. In the book of Exodus when Moses was leading the people through the wilderness, his father-in-law gave him a wonderful piece of advice. He told him to make captains over ten, and captains over 50 and hundreds and thousands, and etc. and then if the people could not work things after following certain procedures, then to bring their problems before Moses.

I know this is on a greater scale, but the principle remains the same. One person cannot do everything whether it's in the home, in a business, or in a ministry. Shortly after this, I began to delegate specific job duties and responsibilities to others whom the Lord had sent to the ministry. Sadly, a few employees who were not promoted began to second guess me and a newly appointed supervisor. I saw this, but felt alone in the battle. I knew that I wasn't equipped in this area. I was in a position I was not truly prepared for and I needed some help. But my trust in leadership had been broken. I watched decisions and choices made that were both unethical and deeply disappointing—decisions that blurred the line between personal gain and professional duty.

I recognized that there needed to be a change, the learning center had not been built on a firm foundation, the staff has gotten out of control. Repentance was needed! But there was no repentance. I tried to implement consequences, but those consequences were often undercut. There was a bump here and a crack there, and I saw them and I tried to patch them up and smooth them over, but the bumps and cracks eventually returned. It was total and complete chaos.

It's like when you build a house and put-up drywall; the walls are so smooth. Now compare this to a house that is being rehabilitated and the walls have holes in them and a contractor goes in and repairs the walls; they are never as smooth as the walls when they are built brand new. I had a few truly good people who tried to help me smooth out the cracks and fill in the holes, but the cracks and holes eventually came back. And you know how cracks and holes are; things can crawl through cracks and holes that are not supposed to creep through the walls. Like roaches, for example, when one roach gets through the cracks, you know that there are hundreds to follow.

It happened the same way at the learning center. We went through a period where staff was coming and going; it was a revolving door. And the enemy was right there in the midst. The center was filled with rebellion—people doing what they wanted to when they wanted to. There was no order, and with each passing day, I felt like I was digging myself deeper in the hole. Have you ever felt like you've been just hanging on for so long that trying to stand up and make a change seems pointless? That is the way I felt. The enemy filled my head with thoughts of giving in and walking away. The noises kept saying, "Why are you trying to set rules now? We've been doing it this way since I started. Why should I change now?" I tried confiding in loved ones, but the answers I received left me feeling even more defeated. I was physically exhausted.

Just when I thought I couldn't take it anymore; the Lord sent a wonderful retired school teacher to the Learning Center. I promoted her to the Assistant Director position to work in collaboration with the Supervisor. We were back on track—at least for the time being. She helped me tremendously. She came in early and worked late. She brought a lot to the program, but there was still some house cleaning that I needed to do.

Every Monday morning, we would start the week off with devotion. The teachers and the children would come together in one of the classrooms to pray, read a scripture, and briefly discuss it. On one particular Monday devotion, I read the scripture and asked if anyone wanted to explain what the scripture meant to the children. One of the younger teachers asked if she could explain it. She wasn't well versed in the bible, but I thought that she did a good job and she spoke from her heart. Then another teacher stood up, condemned the younger teacher, told her that she didn't know what she was talking about, and that if she was going to explain a scripture, she should make sure she had her facts straight. I couldn't believe my ears. Within minutes, the entire teaching staff was hollering back and forth at each other in front of the children. It was at that particular moment that I knew the enemy was on a mission to destroy what God had ordained. It had nothing to do with me—it was an attempt to interfere with spreading the Gospel. Lives were being changed; families were coming to Christ, and his job was to tear it down.

I dismissed everyone back to their classrooms and walked to my office to pray. While sitting there, the Lord had me turn in my bible to the book of Ephesians

> **Finally, my brethren, be strong in the Lord, and in the power of his might. Put on the whole armour of God, that ye may be able to stand against the wiles of the devil. For we wrestle not against flesh and blood, but against principalities, against powers, against the rulers of the darkness of this world, against spiritual wickedness in high places. (Ephesians 6: 10-12).**

It was a spiritual battle I was trying to fight it in the natural. I called my assistant and staff supervisor to the office, and I told them that we were going to anoint every classroom and every piece of furniture in the center. We prayed and I asked God to send His Holy Spirit and let His Spirit rule and reign in the center. We also prayed and commanded everything that was not like God to leave the center. I asked God to remove them.

We walked through the classrooms and took authority over every demonic spirit that had infiltrated its way in the center. After that I went home. My assistant called me and told me that the staff was talking about running me off. I told her that it was ok and not to worry. God will take care of it. The following morning the one teacher who attacked the younger teacher at the devotion did not show up for work. She quit. Within the next few weeks two other teachers walked out. They claimed that I was impartial, and did not treat everyone equally. I said to myself, "Thank you Jesus." He worked it out. I didn't have to do a thing except watch God move.

But of course, Satan didn't let up. All was well for nearly a year. Then I got a phone call late one Sunday night. My assistant was taken to the hospital; she had suffered a heart attack. She passed within a month, and I felt like the weight of the center was back on my shoulders again.

21 THE BREAKING POINT

I kept my purse in the bottom drawer of my desk. The drawer did not lock and I didn't normally lock my office door because this was a Christian daycare. I took my comb out of my purse and went to the restroom to comb my hair. When I returned to the office, I put my comb back and I had a funny feeling in the pit of my stomach. Something told me to look in my wallet. I know now that it was the Holy Spirit. Anyway, when I looked in my wallet, my driver's license and credit card were missing. As I was looking through my purse, one of the teachers had a group of children in the restroom directly across the office. I noticed her looking at me. Instantly, the Holy Spirit revealed to me that she was one of the teachers who stole the items from my purse. There was another teacher, whom she had recently become very good friends with, who served as her accomplice. I never said a word to either of them personally, but I knew.

I did call a staff meeting and announced that some items were stolen from my purse. I informed the staff that from now on I wanted all purses locked in cabinets. We purchased and installed cabinets, and of course it was the talk of the center for the next few days. Everyone was trying to figure out who had done it, but naturally, no one came clean and admitted it. I did call my credit card company and report my card stolen and closed my account before any purchases were made. Thank the Lord. But I failed to report my driver's license stolen to the police. I was naïve; I couldn't imagine what anyone could do with my driver's license.

How wrong was I. I had forgot all about the incident until my husband and I were getting ready to buy a new house. We received a copy of our credit report and found out that someone had stolen my identity and rented an apartment, had the gas, telephone, and cable turned on under my name. This person had run the bills up so high and then vanished. It was a nightmare. I had to go through so much drama to try to clear my name. First, I filed a police report. Then I had to contact each of those creditors and explain to them that someone had stolen my social security number and made those debts. I had to write numerous letters and send document after document in an attempt to prove that it wasn't me.

The Lord was really on my side because the mortgage company we were using only required that I write a letter stating that I was not the person in questions and have the letter notarized. We were blessed to be able to close on our house without any problems. For four years I felt like I was on the battlefield. I had loads of ammunition; the full armor of God, but I was getting tired. Episode after episode occurred at the center and I didn't know what else to do. And in addition to the challenges at the center, there were also many challenges at home.

My husband and I have four children and they were keeping me very busy. They still are—even as adults. Between gymnastics, soccer, cheerleading practice, and football games, and track practice, and coming home and trying to cook dinner and keeping the house clean and doing laundry, sometimes I didn't know if I was coming or going. Before the center opened, I wore a size nine, and by the end of the third year, I was down to a size three. I looked anorexic. My fingers and toes began to tingle all through the day, but particularly in the morning. Then the tingling began to spread to my lips. I began to feel nervous and anxious all the time, but especially in the morning when I knew I had to go to work. During the drive to work, my anxiety got stronger and stronger. I also started having panic attacks, and there was no basis for them. Sometimes I would be in my car and suddenly a panic attack would come over me.

I remember on one occasion I was driving on the freeway. I don't remember where I was coming from now, but as I was driving, I became completely disoriented. I didn't know where I was, and I couldn't remember where I was going, and I couldn't figure out how to get home. I got off the freeway on the next exit and pulled off on the side of the road. I called my husband on my cell phone, and told him I don't know where I was or how I got there. He asked me to look for a street sign and to tell him what building or landmark was nearby. After calming down, he explained to me how to get home. I knew I had to make some changes.

I made a doctor's appointment, and my doctor began doing test after test after test. They took so much blood, that my arms were beginning to feel sore. I thought I was dying. I remember laying on my bed at home one afternoon. I was so weak. My children came into the bedroom and saw me laying there, and they began to cry. I recall my youngest daughter saying, "Mommy, I don't want you to die." Trying to be strong for her, I said, "Oh I'm not gonna die sweetie; I'm just tired." But I thought I was. When all the test results came back, they couldn't find anything wrong. The doctor told me that they had taken every possible blood test, and he didn't know what else he could do for me. I was determined I was not going to give up until I had some answers and I started to cry.

It was like out of nowhere, the doctor asked me, "Have you been crying a lot lately?" When he said that I just broke down and lost it. I began to cry uncontrollably. He told me to wait a minute. He had one more test for me to take. When he walked back in the room, he had a piece of paper and a pencil. I looked at him like he was crazy. He explained to me that he wanted me to answer the questions on the paper. Some of the questions were: Have you been feeling uncommonly sad? Do you find yourself crying for no apparent reason? Do you seem to get more frustrated that normal? Does your heart beat abnormally fast most of the time? As I began answering the questions, I noticed my response to every question was, yes.

When I finished taking the test, the doctor took the answer sheet and left the office. When he returned, he told me that based on my test results it pointed to depression and anxiety disorder, possibly caused by stress or a chemical imbalance in my brain. At last, I was getting some answers. The doctor gave me a two-week sample of an anti-depressant, but he explained that the medication alone was not enough. He told me that I was wearing myself too thin, and that I needed to sit down and prioritize how I was spending my time. He suggested I sit down with the children and decide what activities were most important to them and focus only on those. He also suggested that I reduce my responsibilities at the center. I didn't see how I could reduce my responsibilities; everything that I did was just a part of being the Executive Director of the center.

A good friend of mine, who was a Minister at the church, dropped by the center a few days later to see how I was doing. Isn't it amazing how God works? He did not know what I was going through; he just showed up. I asked him if he would pray with me. I had come to the conclusion that I was going to have to quit. I had spoken to my husband, and he wanted me to put all the cards on the table and tell the Pastor everything, but like I always do, I thought I could just handle it on my own. Anyway, while praying, my friend told me that he could see me standing inside of a box. I was moving my arms as if I was trying to get out, but I couldn't. It was at that moment when the Lord gave me the assignment to write my story. Before this time, I never looked at situations where I felt trapped with no outlets as boxes before. After our prayer, I knew that I had to get out of the box, but I didn't know how. It took four long years of standing, until finally I lay prostrate before my maker and said, "Lord, help me bust out of this thing!"

In 1998, when I went on maternity leave after my son was born, I didn't step completely away. A few weeks after delivery, I was already back at my computer—tracking time and attendance, processing payroll, and managing two of the organization's largest federal grants. I wasn't in the office, but I was still carrying the weight of the work. So, when a report was presented at the church board meeting that I was being paid "to answer questions," it stung deeper than I expected. My uncle, who was sitting in the room that day, called my mother upset. He said the way it was shared, made it seem like I was being paid to sit at home and do nothing. And then he said something that stopped me cold: *"Be careful."* His words settled heavy on my heart—because I knew exactly what he meant. The truth was being twisted, and the room I trusted was shifting beneath my feet—not aware of the truth.

The last four years—from 2000 to 2004—were the hardest of all. I watched the board chair make choices that were both unethical and deeply disappointing—decisions that blurred the line between personal gain and professional duty. The breaking point came with two incidents I could no longer overlook: the first, when he misappropriated money to invest in a pyramid scheme for personal gain, and the second, when his mishandling of taxes prompted an internal investigation by the Department of Labor. What hurt most wasn't just his actions, but his refusal to take responsibility. Instead, he shifted the blame and made remarks that called my character into question. That was the moment I knew I could no longer stay.

Seeking some sense of understanding, I shared my feelings with someone I loved, hoping to be seen and supported. Instead, their response left me unmoored—far from the reassurance I had hoped for. Frustration and quiet anger settled over me, mingling with the deep feeling of sadness, and for a moment, completely alone in my disappointment. The anger and resentment had taken root in me, forming a stronghold I came to call my Steel Box. Earlier, I mentioned how the soldered ends of steel are even stronger than the steel itself. That's what my depression became—the solder that sealed my box shut. The anger and bitterness I carried fed the depression, binding me inside something stronger than I ever imagined.

That little girl who once raced home from school in tears—the same young woman who felt abandoned by friends—rose up in me again, carrying those old feelings of loneliness, disappointment, and betrayal. And just like before, instead of turning to God, I found myself slipping back into old habits, reaching for alcohol to numb the pain I was unable to face.

After my initial diagnosis, it wasn't easy to talk about. In the black community, mental health wasn't a topic discussed. My mom would tell me, "Just get out the bed—just pray." I did pray, but I needed more. My depression and anxiety were believed to be caused by stress, a lack of rest and a chemical imbalance. I stand today knowing that, yes, a chemical imbalance is a real and proven medical condition, but the enemy will take advantage of the times when we are physically and mentally the weakest, and attack our minds and bodies.

I remember when I was a little girl, my mom would always tell my brother and I to make sure we ate right. She would say, "Your body is just like a car, you can't expect it to run if you don't keep gasoline in it." I will go even further to say that we change the breaks in our cars, change the oil, give them tune-ups, etc. We should do the same thing with our bodies. Not only should we make sure that we eat, but we need to eat the right foods and proper proportions. We need protein, vegetables, fruits, dairy products, grains, and even a small number of sugars and fats. Our bodies also require adequate rest and exercise. A lack of sleep causes irritability, and it also affects our thinking process. When your body is tired, it disrupts your concentration and focus. It also affects your ability to stand strong and make sound decisions.

A prime example of this is when children have to take a test for school. Their teacher always instructs them to get a good night's sleep and to eat a good breakfast the day of the test. When you are well rested and ready to start the day with a healthy meal, your brain is also well rested, and the information that is stored in it is easily retrieved.

The same thing applies to our spirit man. When our body is constantly being worn down, and our minds are relentlessly filled with enmity, we might find it more difficult to keep our spirit man lifted up. I know for me, this was, and probably is still one of my most difficult challenges. I will state again that the enemy cannot touch our spirit, but Paul writes in I Corinthians, "I die daily." We must crucify our flesh every day. Also in Galatians 6:7-8 Paul states, "Be not deceived; God is not mocked: for whatsoever a man soweth, that shall he also reap. For he that soweth to his flesh shall of the flesh reap corruption; be he that soweth to the Spirit shall of the Spirit reap life everlasting."

After reaching those words I began to meditate on what Paul actually meant. I pictured Paul waking up every morning and making a conscious decision to crucify his flesh each day-taking one day at a time. First it takes spiritual revelation knowledge that reveals to us that we are in a spiritual battle. Once our spirit man recognizes the enemy, the information goes to our minds and then finally we act things out in the natural. Paul's spirit revealed to him the concept of crucifying his flesh in the spirit first, then he understood it in his mind, finally he took steps to act it out in the natural. Whether he woke up every day and prayed or read the Bible or whatever, it was a physical act.

Likewise, today, all acts of the flesh, whether good or bad first begins in our mind. So, sowing to the flesh begins first with a thought about the flesh. Whether it is something we see on television, or see at the theater, or read in a book, or a thought that we don't cast down, those thoughts can be given life and then manifested in the flesh. When you really think about it, sin begins with a thought in our minds. We must learn to take control of our minds and what we allow our minds to think on. Just like we make an effort to eat right and exercise, we have to make an effort to feed our minds And exercise our minds with the Word of God which goes directly to our Spirit man.

Philippians 2:5 says, "Let this mind be in you, which was also in Christ Jesus." We should desire to have the mind of Christ. We know that Jesus lived a perfect life while he was on the Earth. He was without sin. But this doesn't mean that he wasn't tempted and that the enemy did not try to attack his mind. We know that he did. For example, when Jesus was led by the Spirit into the wilderness, he was tempted of the devil for forty days in Luke 4. First the devil tempted him with a physical need. He told Jesus to command a stone to be made bread. Jesus responded by saying, "It is written that man shall not live by bread alone, but by every word of God" (Matthew 4:4). Next, the devil tempted him with material possessions and worldly power. The devil took Jesus up into a high mountain and showed him all the kingdoms of the world in a moment of time. The devil told him that he would give him all this power if he would worship him. Jesus answered by saying, "Get thee behind me Satan: for it is written, thou shalt worship the Lord thy God and him only shalt thou serve" (Matthew 4:10). Finally, the devil tempted Jesus in the area of safety and protection. The devil set Jesus on a pinnacle of the temple and told him to cast himself down from it if he truly was the Son of God. The devil even quoted the word to Jesus in an attempt to deceive him. Again, Jesus reminded him not to tempt God. When the devil stopped trying to tempt Him, he left, but it was only for a season.

What can we learn from this? First off, we see that the devil tempted Jesus by talking to him. Jesus had to have heard him, and if that be the case, then the words had to have entered Jesus' mind. Now the devil may not talk to us directly, but he will use other people to talk to us and tell us things in an attempt to get us off focus. The devil tempted Jesus with a physical need. Jesus hadn't eaten for forty days so he was hungry. Bear in mind that a physical temptation may not necessarily be for food. It could also be sex, cigarettes, drugs and alcohol, or food. How did Jesus respond. He didn't allow the words to stay in his mind, but he cast them down and quoted what the word said about his situation.

Secondly, Jesus not only used words to tempt Jesus, he also used Jesus' sense of sight. He told him he would give him power, but he also showed him all the kingdoms of the world. We know that images we see enter into our minds. In Jesus case, he was offered land and earthly power. For us, we may be tempted to take a job that is not God's best for us. We may get into an enormous amount of debt because we make unwise purchases, in order to keep up with the Jones'. I believe this was a mental temptation. In this world today, we are often judged by the amount of money we have, the type of job we have, and where we live. It makes us feel good in our minds when we are successful and when we are respected in the world. But remember, only what we do for Christ will last. We see that Jesus used the written word to resist the temptation and to sow to the spirit and not the flesh.

In the last temptation, the devil tried to use God's own words against him. This was a spiritual temptation because the devil quoted the word. There are times when people use God's word out of context, or to fit their own situation. And we have to use discernment to determine what is right and wrong, and what to do in certain circumstances. God expects us to use wisdom in making decisions. The scripture does say that he shall give his angels charge over us, but we cannot expect God to intercede in a situation where we knowingly walked into just to prove a point that God can deliver us. For example, someone who has recently been delivered from alcoholism should not keep beer or wine in his/her refrigerator just to prove that they have enough willpower to resist taking a drink. Likewise, someone who is struggling with fornication shouldn't allow himself to be alone in a room with someone of the opposite sex, to show that God can give him a way of escape. Finally, we see again that Jesus spoke the written word.

In every temptation, Jesus knew what words to speak in each situation. In order for us to know what scripture to use, we must know the scriptures. Second Timothy 2:15 says: Study to shew thyself approved unto God, a workman that needed not to be ashamed, rightly dividing the word of truth. My understanding of this verse tells me that first off, we need to study the word. We study, not only to know the word for ourselves, but also to seek God's approval. We must study to learn how to rightly divide the word. What does that mean? It means to get a correct understanding of the word and the right interpretation of the word. And not only that, but understanding how God's word, all fits together. And when we understand the word correctly, then we don't need to be ashamed, because we have the correct interpretation. When we teach others or attempt to explain the word to others, it pleases God, and we gain his approval. How can we teach others about God and his word when we don't rightly divide the word ourselves?

In the year 2000, the center had tripled in capacity. I hired a full-time Administrator to run the day-to-day operations so I would be able to focus on business operations, federal grants, contracts, and the organization's social enterprise. I was able to do more training and more ministry work. Children gave their lives to Christ; families came to know Jesus when their children shared what they were learning at preschool. God was at work. The attacks were not aimed at me, but at the work God was doing through me and that ministry.

It was April 29, 2001 when the Lord spoke to me and told me that he was going to use me to minister to teenage girls and young women. I was in the restroom at church one Sunday morning. Four teenage girls were also in the restroom. One of the girls was changing her baby's diaper. I overheard one of the girls asking the girl who was changing the infant if she and her baby's daddy were still together. She explained to them that she had another boyfriend now, and that her friend was going out with her baby's daddy now.

My heart went out to those young women. They talked as if it wasn't a big deal. To go from relationship to relationship without any sense of commitment is the norm in today's society. Fornication is no longer viewed as sin to the majority of the population, and it's time we get back to holiness. I gladly accepted the call, and I was excited about it. It was then that my challenges began to increase.

I began to really dig into the word, and study everything I could about holiness, and our bodies being temples, and marriage and covenants. And as I studied the Lord began to give me topics on other subject matters as well. Some scriptures that I had studied before or read before were brought back to my remembrance, and the Lord began giving me a different understanding of them. It seemed that week after week I was getting a new topic from God. He instructed me, through the Spirit of course, to begin writing them down, so I did. After a few months I began praying and asking God what he wanted me to do with this information. He told me to just store them up.

I felt as close to God as I have ever been in my life. I desired to become even closer, but for me it felt good. I felt that God trusted me, and that he was entrusting me with knowledge that I would be given an opportunity to share at the appointed time. I studied and felt at peace for nearly two years. My family was doing well, my marriage was at one of its highest points. My husband even noticed a difference in our marriage. He told me that this is how he had always imagined a marriage should be. And then it all started to change.

It seemed that once I realized what my true calling was, and still is, and made a decision to truly live for God, and to work towards and live for my calling, that Satan began attacking me more than I had ever been attacked before. Near the end of 2003, October or November, I found myself slipping further into depression and struggling weekly with anxiety and daily panic attacks.

It would start early in the morning. Some days, it took every ounce of strength just to get out of bed. And even after sleeping eight hours, I found myself waking up still completely exhausted. After the children would leave for school, I would get dressed for the day. Some days I would go to work, and others I would lay around the house crying and longing for more out of life. I felt like I was just going through the motions. Even though I knew for the first time in my life that I wanted to write more than anything in the world, and nothing made me happier or more satisfied, I felt that fulfilling that dream of mine was an unlikely reality. I felt useless and worthless, and thought my life was pointless.

On days when I would go to work, I did feel better for the moment. Sometimes the work would overwhelm me, even though my job was not extremely demanding. Budget issues brought me down, having a deadline brought me down, having to go to a meeting brought me down, having to contact a parent for information brought me down. Neither of those things required much effort, but having to do them would send me into a deep depression. I didn't want to do it anymore, even though I felt inside that I was supposed to be there. I remember receiving a memo from one of our partnership organizations informing me of a mandatory meeting the following week. For the entire period leading up to that meeting, I felt intense stress, anxiety and depression. But there was no reason for it. I didn't have to do anything special for the meeting, I didn't have to stand up and talk—nothing—but it overwhelmed me.

When I would return home from work, I had a usual routine. I would either go upstairs in my bedroom and lay down, or I would retreat to the living room and lay down on the couch. I couldn't get motivated to do anything. The house needed cleaning, the floor needed swept, dishes needed washed, clothes need laundered, dinner needed preparing, instead I did nothing but sleep. In my heart I wanted to cook and clean, but my body wouldn't allow me. I felt utterly fatigued. And naturally, my feelings spilled over into my family life.

My two youngest children would come home from school and they would find me laying on the couch in the living room. They wanted to share with me about their day and they needed help with their homework, but all I could do was lay there listlessly. And you know how innocent and sweet children are, and how they love so unconditionally. They would ask me, "Are you tired mommy? You don't feel well?" I would usually answer them by saying, "No, mommy's not feeling too good right now." Sometimes they would sit on the couch beside me and rub my back, or just lay there silently beside me for fifteen or twenty minutes. Eventually they would go into the kitchen and work on their homework on their own and fix themselves a peanut butter and jelly sandwich or ramen noodles until I could get up.

Some days were better than others; some days I would sleep for nearly two or three hours—others, only fifteen or twenty minutes. No matter how long I slept, when I was awake, I still was mentally separate from the children. I tried to reach out to a loved one for help, but the usual comment was, "You're tough, you can handle it." or "Be strong, it's just the devil, shake it off." or "You're spiritual, you know the word." And even though all those things were true, I was strong, I knew that I was under attack from the devil, and yes, I knew the word, but that is not what I wanted to hear. I wanted to know that I was loved—that someone was there for me and that I was significant. Instead of looking to God, who is our refuge and strength, a very present help in trouble, I looked to man. (Psalm 46:1). My anger grew and resentment settled. What I expected didn't happen, but even worse, my expectations, I did not communicate. I was ready to give up on everything—marriage, work, life! This was now April 2004.

I knew it was time to leave when my anger and frustration hardened into something darker. I remember sitting in church, and whenever a certain board member walked past me—or stopped by our pew to speak—I felt hatred rise in my chest. It scared me. Hate began to consume me, shaping my thoughts, my worship, even my breathing. And I hated that my loved one didn't feel the same hate. What I expected, I did not see. And I didn't want to be that person. I prayed with everything in me for the Lord to remove the hate from my heart. I fasted. I cried. I begged. But the grip of it stayed. That anger I tried so hard to hide, became fuel for a depression I didn't have the words for at the time. I kept asking myself, *how could I, who says I love God, carry so much anger inside?* What began as disappointment—sadness, slowly turned into frustration… then anger… then hate. And eventually, depression and anxiety wrapped themselves around my life.

I carried that hate in my heart for nearly fifteen years. Some days I managed. Some seasons were lighter than others. But no matter how steady I felt during the week, Sunday always came—and with it the weight of knowing I would have to face my own pain again. The anxiety would rise before I even walked into the sanctuary, tightening around me, like a reminder that I was still bleeding on the inside.

I resigned from the learning center in July, 2004. Looking back, each year from 1996 on seemed to grow heavier, more discouraging than the last. My experiences weren't all bad. In fact, there were far more good moments than difficult ones, and that's what kept me there for eight years—along with the unspoken pressure I felt to stay. How I could walk away from something I had poured my heart into for so long?

Those eight years held some of the most beautiful moments of my life. I watched children and their families give their hearts to Christ and saw little ones experience the love of God in ways that touched me deeply. I prayed with young adults and parents who were struggling, and together we found comfort in His presence. Our Christmas plays, joyful; our annual holiday dinners felt like big family gathering. In between my silent pain there were moments of light—small acts of kindness, laughter echoing down the halls, and glimpses of God's grace in the faces of the children. Those moments were the things that kept my heart anchored—even when my spirit felt weary.

OUT OF THE BOX
A Day in Depression
Dubonna L Dawkins

I awaken and note that the sun is still shining luminously
Although to me darkness seems to have overtaken any
Shimmer of light
A cloud of heaviness weighs forcefully on my heart. Penetrating so mightily as to limit the otherwise
Normal flow of blood

Trying to pull my lifeless body away from the comfort of my bed; Limbs so exhausted from the endless anxiety that
Controls me even in sleep
Hoping that each new day will be the day when the cycle will cease; Praying that the Everlasting Father will show
His mercy to me

Longing to feel normal yet not knowing what normal truly is
Only knowing that what I feel, surely cannot be
As the day slowly passes, only fragments of sanity enter my windows; The gateway to my soul where the enemy has tried to Control from within

I fight until it's night…still not knowing the truth
Which lies behind the pain
Feeling despondent and unfulfilled, incomplete, complacent,
And weary, but through it all, trusting that one day I will
Awaken and see the sun still hanging brightly in the sky and shining Boldly upon me

The darkness will have faded away and only the most brilliant light glows, and joy fills my heart once more and extraordinary yet again. I will be.

22 A WOMB NOT EASILY HEALED

During my eight years at the Learning Center, I had a series of wonderful memories, periods of growth, lessons only taught through experiences, and insights that taught me that vulnerability often comes with pain and strength only comes through trials. Repeated betrayal fostered a deep reluctance to trust, past disillusionments instilled in me a fear of dependence, and through loss and disappointment, I learned emotional self-sufficiency. What I called self-sufficiency was really self-protection. I fled from conflict because facing it felt like risking trust. My self-reliance became a shield; instead of standing my ground in conflict, I withdrew. In trying to depend on no one, I ended up running from the very moments that required connection and courage.

I lost count of how many jobs I held over the next five years. Some lasted six months, others only a few weeks; a couple barely made it past a handful of days—and one, I think, ended after just a single day. Each time a challenge arose, fear took over—the fear of reliving the pain I'd already endured—I fled before it could happen again. I'd learned not to speak about it, afraid of being misunderstood or dismissed, so I buried it instead. Running and self-medications became my coping mechanism—my pain-numbing medicine. If only for a moment—it became my survival.

I continued visiting my family doctor—fairly regularly—along with taking my anti-depressants. The endless amount of sleeping did lessen, but my feelings of loneliness and isolation continued. I went through periods of medication non-adherence because I believed the treatment wasn't working. My doctor consistently adjusted my medications, trying to find the combination that worked best for me. Nevertheless, I didn't give any combination of medications enough time to see if they really worked.

Gradually I saw myself turning away from God and giving up the fight. I loved the Lord with all my heart, but found myself spending less and less time with Him. I became a different person. I truly believe "my house" was invaded. What do I mean by "my house"? My physical body, emotions, and specifically, my mind. Looking at the scripture in Second Timothy 3:6 which says, "For of this sort are they which creep into houses, and lead captive silly women laden with sins, led away with divers' lusts." What did Timothy mean by "of this sort"? I believe he meant people who had allowed spirits of anti-Christ: disobedience to God's word, false prophets, confusion, perversion, etc. to infiltrate their spirit man. These same people have a tremendous amount of influence and persuasion, usually subliminal, on people: believers and unbelievers. You might ask how do they creep into houses? Through the media: television, radio, magazines, books. Or the influence may be direct. It could be people we allow ourselves to associate with.

How can a true believer who loves the Lord and is filled with the Holy Ghost allow an unclean spirit to creep into his house? A small crack in the wall. Sometimes a crack can be so small that you can't even see it and you don't even realize it's there until it begins to spread. How is a crack formed in a wall? It could be from years of wear or possibly from a sudden blow. My house (mind) was crept into through a small crack that I didn't patch up quickly when it first appeared. The first sign and symptom of depression I experienced should have been squashed, stomped on, and cast down immediately. I didn't respond to the test that way. Remember I stated earlier that I knew it would be a fight and I didn't want to fight. I gave in. Any by giving in, I allowed the crack to spread, and once it started spreading, it spread quickly.

As I mentioned earlier, I saw myself gradually turning away from God. It started when I spent less and less time in prayer and reading and studying the Word. I attributed it to the fact that I was always so tired from the depression and anxiety, but that was no excuse. Yes, I was exhausted and my exhaustion was a real symptom triggered by excessive beating of the heart caused by the anxiety attacks. Still, even when you're tired you must persevere. Psalm 27:1 says, "The Lord is the strength of my life." Psalm 29:11 says, "The Lord will give strength unto his people." Being tired is the time when we should look to the Lord. Only he can give us strength when we are weary.

It was like a ripple effect in my life. I then stopped tithing, didn't want to wake up and go to church, stopped singing in the Sprit (something that I loved to do), and eventually I felt lifeless. I recall telling my mother that I felt like I was dreaming. I felt as if I was merely going through the motions every day. I was living to die. And to top it off, Satan then attacked my physical body.

I began having horrific cramping in my lower abdomen and began bleeding from my rectum after having bowel movements. I was afraid to tell anyone, so I kept it all inside for close to a month. Eventually the fear overwhelmed me and I told my husband. I went to our family doctor and he decided to schedule me for a series of tests. First my physician arranged for an ultra sound the following week to see what could be causing the abdominal cramping. The results of this test showed no signs of abnormality. Second, he scheduled me to have a colonoscopy two weeks later. During the two weeks prior to the test date, I recall a conversation I had with the Lord. Yes, I said conversation. I was taking a shower one evening and I began sobbing uncontrollably. I asked God, "What's wrong with me? Do I have cancer? Am I going to have to have enough faith to drive cancer out of my body?" So sweetly and gently, the Lord spoke to me and said, "No, DuBonna, you don't have cancer." This calmed me for a moment. Then I asked God again, "Well, what do I have?" He answered me again, "You don't have anything."

I had to question Him deeper, "So what's going on with me?" Then the Lord reminded me of the story of Job. He explained to me that Satan had gotten permission from Him to inflict Job, and that Satan had gotten permission from Him to afflict me with symptoms. The Lord also told me that He told Satan he was limited to what he put on me. Can you imagine how thrilled I was? The Lord loved me so much that he allowed these symptoms to come in my body to get my attention. God wanted me to do a work for Him and he was waiting for me to submit and declare, "Lord, let your will be done in my life. No matter what it is." I thought I was finally ready for the fight that was before me so I made a decision to not take the colonoscopy test.

For the two weeks that followed, I did nothing but read and study the Word, listened to sermons on tape, watched Christian television, sang in the Spirit, prayed in the Spirit, and quoted scriptures all day long. My mom gave me some herbal teas and supplements which I took religiously. I knew the enemy was attacking me and I fought with tooth and nail and the Lord delivered me. The pain in my lower abdomen stopped and the bleeding stopped. The Lord proved Himself again. He loves me; His Word is true and, He cannot go back on His promises.

I was so busy fighting against the attack on my physical body, that I didn't have time to be anxious or depressed. My Spirit man was constantly being fed and my soul (mind) was actively searching for proof in the Word of God that healing was for me. But as soon as healing was manifested in my body, I stopped pressing in on the Word. I couldn't grasp why it was so difficult for me to believe God for deliverance from the oppression in my mind. That is what depression and anxiety and paranoia is, an oppressive spirit.

One day while walking out of a bank, the security officer asked me if he could talk to me for a minute. I asked him what this was about? He then asked me if I was a *First Lady*? I told him that I wasn't. He then told me that I had the spirit of a *First Lady* and that he could see I was under attack.

I knew the Lord, loved the Lord, and knew that I was under attack. What was revealed to the security guard was confirmation. I knew what I was supposed to do, and I knew the tools needed to do it, and I was equipped with them, but I knew it would be a fight, and I didn't have the strength to fight. Fighting takes effort, time, strength, energy, and consistency. Even in the spirit realm, a fight is still a fight. The enemy had convinced my mind that I wasn't strong, that I didn't really have a purpose and call for my life, and that my life was not worth fighting for.

The depression was constant. I was visiting my family doctor pretty regularly and continuing on my anti-depressants. The endless amount of sleeping did lessen, but my feelings of loneliness and isolation continued. I was writing more—a passion that helped me put my thoughts into words I could not say aloud. I was looking for a job, but knew with my mental health, it wouldn't last long.

Then one day I was looking in the newspaper for job openings and saw an ad for coaching vacancies. A few high schools were hiring for head and assistant girls' track coaches. For the first time in years, I felt like a door had opened for me to do something that I genuinely loved. I was blessed with the assistant girls' track coach position at a public high school in the city. I was so excited, but unfortunately not everyone shared my enthusiasm.

My parents, especially my mom, was concerned about my children and how they would be cared for after school, and rightfully so. I had the same concerns because I knew my priority was to my children and not a track team, but it was a job and I needed it for me. My husband was concerned about the amount of gasoline it would take to travel back and forth to the track each day, as it was not close to my home. And yes, he had a valid concern as well, but to me the positive outweighed the negative without comparison. My dad helped out a lot and would meet my kids at my house when they got from school and take them to his house, and on a few occasions my mom did as well, but I still felt as if I were imposing on others which left me feeling burdensome. And every time the gas tank had to be filled up again, I had to hear the never-ending gasps of disapproval and incontinent. Despite the opposition, I finished two seasons and I felt good about it.

I think it was then when I realized that it was ok for me to me happy; that my life did not just center around my children and husband. For so many women, we so often times lose sight of who we are and forget that we are people too with feelings and emotions. We are more than just mothers who transport their children to track practice, and cheerleading, and soccer and basketball. We are more than wives who try their darnedest to keep the house clean and prepare dinner and cater to their spouse's needs. We are also women with feelings and needs and desires.

I saw myself changing, but found it difficult to communicate my feelings to the people in my life and especially to the ones I loved the most. It seemed that the more I tried to express my feelings, the more resistance I got and the more frustration I felt. Now looking back on it, I don't believe it was resistance, but misunderstanding. It was new to all of us, and we all needed to work together. I wanted more out of life. The everyday routine of waking up and getting the kids off to school and going to work and coming home and cooking dinner and helping with homework and watching the nightly line up on television and going to bed had gotten old......too old.

It was a roller coaster—going from moments of high to moments of low. Thoughts of my death began to creep back in. I didn't want to die, but I believed I was going to die. I was overwhelmed with a fear that I had a deadly disease and my life would soon be over. I was not sick; I had not been diagnosed with anything; I had not been to the doctor, but I had lost a significant amount of weight because I couldn't eat or sleep, due to a fear that I was dying. I struggled with depression and used alcohol to self-medicate. I went through a period where I drank every day—anything to dull the pain. I drank until I feel asleep, got up the next morning and did it all over again.

One day I was reminded of a conversation I had with my mother and she had told me about a preacher who pastored a church on the North side of Columbus. I recalled my mom telling me how this pastor had prayed with one of my cousins who was struggling with alcohol abuse. She mentioned that he shared that people with Native Americans in their genealogy have issues with alcohol abuse and don't know the source and the history behind it. I remember walking in the church and the odor was so strong, smelling of mildew, like a damp basement after a flood. I recognized this odor because my childhood home flooded often after a hard rain, causing the odor to seek upstairs for weeks after the waters subsided.

I wondered through a few doors, not seeing anyone in the church when a woman asked what I needed. I told her that I wanted to speak with the pastor and that my mom had brought a cousin here and he had prayed for her. She walked me to another room and the pastor greeted me. He asked me why I had come and I began to share. He asked me my genealogy and if I knew if my grandparents or great grandparents were Native American. I told him that I had a great grandfather or great-great grandfather, who was called Indian Charlie.

From a biblical perspective, the disproportionate struggles with alcohol among some Native American communities are not caused by race, but rather seen through the lenses of the destructive legacy of colonialism. The role of colonial history and actions of European colonizers who used alcohol as a tool of oppression represent a grave moral failing. Europeans deliberately introduced distilled, potent alcohol into Indigenous communities that had little prior exposure to it.

In contrast to traditional fermented beverages used ceremonially, the more powerful alcohol served as a profitable trade good and a tool of "diplomacy" to exploit Native Americans.

According to the American Journal of Public Health (2020), The introduction of alcohol coincided with devastating historical trauma, including violence, land theft, and forced assimilation. Some Native American Christian perspectives see alcohol abuse as a manifestation of this colonial "curse," a tool of violence acted out against one's own people and oneself. A Christian-based recovery paths focus on turning from the idolatry of addiction and seeking fulfillment through a relationship with God. This process includes prayer, community support, and trusting in God's power for transformation.

Although my struggle with depression and anxiety didn't suddenly go away after prayer and the laying on of hands, the knowledge I gained in that experience was a starting point in my understanding the root underneath my challenges.

Silenced
Dubonna Dawkins

Voices silenced by ones who oppose
Oppose merely by reason of fear

Fear of unspoken thoughts and beliefs
Beliefs in inequality and subliminal intolerance

Intolerance to production and promotion
Promotion toward betterment

Betterment mobilized to empowerment
Empowerment gained by knowledge

Knowledge attained through the truth
Truth realized and internalized

Internalized then perpetuated
Perpetuated by voices

Voices that refused to be silenced

23 THE DAY I DIDN'T PUSH THROUGH

Before writing this memoir, I debated on what details I would include. My intention is not to expose others, place blame on anyone, or share too much. However, what I've found is that sharing our story can provide a level of healing that keeping it hidden won't achieve. Sharing can also bring healing to others experiencing the same thing. Hearing someone else's story may allow you to have compassion on yourself—knowing that someone else experienced something similar and overcame.

Even when I tell my story today, people find it hard to believe that I wasn't trying to commit suicide. But I was NOT. I don't remember what lead up to my decision to swallow an entire bottle of pills. I've heard psychologist explain that sometimes our minds forget painful memories as a protective survival mechanism. I don't know if that's true for me or not. I couldn't tell you what led up to my decision, what had happened weeks immediately prior to, or what, if any, experience I had prior to.

I lay on my bed, looking up at the ceiling, got up to take my anti-anxiety medication, which up that point had not been working. I stared at the bottle of pills, opened it and, one by one, swallowed every single one. Moments later, my husband walked in, saw the empty bottle in my hand, and started shouting, "What did you do? Did you take all of these?" The next thing I remember is he is on the phone talking to someone; I'm looking around the bedroom, noticing the colors on the walls; hearing the sound of the emergency squad pulling up in front of the house, listening to footsteps running up the stairway.

Everything after that becomes hazy. The next clear moment I recall is lying in a hospital bed as a woman leaned over and asked why I wanted to end my life by suicide? I answered calmly, "I don't want to die. I didn't try to kill myself." And I meant it. Even now, I know I didn't want to die. I've asked myself countless times why I swallowed that entire bottle, and I still don't have an answer. But what I know for certain is this—I never wanted to die.

The details of that day are a blur, with the exception of the fear on my husband's face, a stranger telling me that I was a threat to myself, and being told that I was being involuntarily committed for 72 hours. I don't remember how I got to Dublin Springs, a behavioral health hospital. I do remember sitting in a small room, feeling interrogated about my overdose, trying to convince anyone who would listen that my intent was not to end my life. Even today, I don't know why I took the pills. I've tried to come up with a rational reason as to why. Was I frustrated that the prescription wasn't strong enough? Was it that I hadn't seen any changes in my mood; was it my attempt to get help? Was it an irrational thought that entered my mind? I don't know.

When admitted, draw strings from my sweatshirts were removed. My shoe laces were taken out. My husband went back home to pack additional items for me. He was instructed not to pack a razor, perfume, or mouthwash—no spiral notebooks or underwire bras.

My memories from those days come in fragments—art therapy, music therapy, the sound of us playing instruments together. Between sessions, I spent hours coloring, journaling, and meeting with counselors and a psychiatrist. Those three days turned into seven when the psychiatrist decided I wasn't ready to leave. Before my release, the hospital connected me with a therapist who would walk with me through many years of recovery. That marked the beginning of my healing journey—the moment I began to break free from the steel box I had been living in.

My diagnoses of depression and anxiety disorder eventually led to three more hospitalizations—the last one being voluntary. It was a long and often painful journey, but it became a path of deep self-discovery. I began to uncover who I truly was, what I believed, and the truth that I couldn't control how others felt or reacted. Accepting that others might not respond the way I expected—or get upset over the same things that angered me—was one of the hardest lessons I've ever learned.

In the years that followed, I accepted a position at another preschool. It was the perfect mix of childcare and human resources. The owners were Christian women and the experience not only allowed me to sharpen my HR skills, it also allowed me to heal—being surrounded by kind and nurturing people. I connected with another woman who had similar dreams as I had—opening her own childcare. Things started to look up again. We formed an LLC and began our journey to open a Christian preschool and nursery.

For the next few years, I did some consulting work while looking for potential locations to open our own childcare. During this time, my father was diagnosed with dementia, which took a toll on my mother. As my dad's dementia deepened, his memory slipped away piece by piece, and with it went the life my parents once knew. My mom tried to hold everything together, but every day grew heavier — neighbors calling to say they'd seen him wandering down the street in his pajamas, moments that were frightening and heartbreaking all at once. Eventually, the weight became more than she could carry alone, and she made the painful decision to place him in a long-term nursing facility. When he passed, it felt like a part of her went with him. Six months later, she followed—two lives bound together, even in goodbye.

My business partner and I were introduced to a young woman whose main work involves connecting aspiring childcare center owners with current owners who are looking to sell. After many months of searching, we found the perfect location. I was able to use a portion of my inheritance as a down payment for the business.

I consulted a family member who was an attorney before making the deposit, but even with that, we ultimately moved forward without doing the proper due diligence. Only later did we discover that the woman who owned the center had a history of lawsuits involving fraud and theft. The situation dragged on in court for months, and in the end, I lost the money. It left me feeling manipulated and deeply disappointed — especially knowing it was money my parents had worked so hard to pass down to my brother and me as an inheritance.

What could have ended in bitterness instead settled into a peace I still can't fully explain. I was devastated, but even in the loss, I felt comfort. I knew it wasn't my place to seek revenge and God would handle what I could not. I recognized that the enemy was trying to destroy me, but God had a plan for me and wanted to use me, it changed my entire outlook on life. I was honoured that God had chosen me. There was nothing special about me. God looks for people who are willing to do as he commands, no matter what. I began to laugh at the enemy. No matter what thoughts he put in my mind, I recognized that he was doing his job, but I also reminded him that he was already defeated. For Proverbs 12:5 says, "The thoughts of the righteous are right." I knew that my thoughts were good. Any thought that came in my mind that was not good, righteous, or uplifting was not my thought. I recognized it for what it was—a lie!

My understanding that humans are both spiritual and physical beings, and this integrated nature means that all aspects of our lives—physical, emotional, and spiritual—are connected and affect each other. For me that consisted of prayer, deliverance, counseling and medication.

The Bible doesn't mention professional counsellors, but it strongly supports the idea of seeking wise counsel and guidance for life's challenges through verses like Proverbs 11:14, which states, "Where no counsel is, the people fall: but in the multitude of counsellors there is safety." Proverbs 1 also emphasizes listening to instruction and receiving advice to become wise. For me, speaking with a Christian counselor who integrated faith into their practice offered support—sharing values, spiritual clarity, and a perspective grounded in biblical principles. My depression resulted from a complex interaction of factors, including genetic vulnerability, trauma, stressful life events, and unresolved anger.

I had always been able to forgive and more forward. I forgave what some might consider a greater act against me—followed by even more devastation. But this time it was different. The thing that pushed me over the edge was when individuals didn't live up to my expectation. It took years to learn that expectations are different for different people—depending on so many things. What I expected was neither right or wrong—it was just my expectation. Other's reactions to things I experienced were neither right or wrong—it was just their reaction.

I learned that it is only God I could truly trust. With man, disappointment always follows. For God is not man, that He should lie. (Numbers 23:19)

24 A FRESH BEGINNING

When we decided to leave Columbus and move to Cincinnati, it felt like taking another step toward healing—closing one chapter and beginning a new one. It was my chance to start over, to leave the past where it belonged. The move wasn't just a change of location; it was a declaration of freedom. And thank God—I truly am free.

The move was easy. My husband had retired. I was doing HR consulting so there were no commitments we needed to concern ourselves with. Our three daughters had graduated college, our son was playing football in Louisville so the drive to his games from Cincinnati was closer. We were happy to be closer to our daughters and grandchildren, who had all relocated to Cincinnati a few years prior.

I found a good job relatively quickly after the move. It was not in human resources, but a challenging role nevertheless. Although life was looking optimistic, there were still occasions of sadness and anxiety, but I had learned to recognize triggers and learned to use coping skills I had gained through therapy. In addition, my medication was regulated and we connected with a church where we continued to grow spiritually.

One of my biggest challenges that took years to overcome, was regulating my thoughts. The mind, better known as our soul, is a part of us that the enemy has used as a powerful weapon for centuries. Whether it's something we see or hear, that information is taken in through our eyes and ears and then processed in our minds. Now what we do with it once it is processed in our minds, is the key to living victoriously or living a defeated life. The mind processes information speedily. And as speedily as it is processed, it must be expelled.

We have two choices. First, we can cast down imaginations and every high thing that elevates itself against the knowledge of God and bring into captivity every thought to the obedience of Christ, as stated in 2 Corinthians 10: 5. Second, we can refuse to cast it down, meditate on it, and eventually act on it. It's not enough to just cast down thoughts and images, we can't meditate on them. We must train our minds to become experts at bringing thoughts and imaginations into captivity. The American Heritage Dictionary defines captivity as, "The state or a period of being captive." Captive is defined as, "One who is forcibly confined, restrained, or subjugated, as a prisoner." We see that bringing something into captivity takes force, involves restraint and control, and involves strong emotion or passion.

When I think about bringing something into captivity, I envision a cage. I see words, thoughts, and emotions being caught in this cage—one that is not only made of the word of God, but encompasses the word. It is only filled with thoughts, emotions, and actions that are obedient to Christ. We have to bring those thoughts into captivity. It doesn't happen automatically and it's not easy. I'll go even further and say that it's probably one of the most difficult actions Christians face daily. Like we have to bring thoughts into captivity, we also have to let them out. They will not flee on their own.

Allow me to use another simple example before I continue. My husband and I bought our first daughter a parakeet for Christmas when she was three years old. My husband used to let the bird out on occasion and allow it to fly around the house. Letting it out was the simple part. All he had to do was merely open the door, and she would fly out. Bringing the bird back into captivity inside that cage was a different matter. I remember him using a towel and sneaking up to the bird and trying to grab it before it would fly away. Some days it took several tries before he could successfully grasp it in the towel, hold on to it and place it back in the cage.

The longer we had the bird, and the more accustomed the bird became of being set free to fly for a short period of time, the easier it got for my husband to catch it and place it back in the cage. Eventually, the bird would fly on his arm willingly when she got tired of flying and he would put her in the cage. Our thought life is the same way. It is so difficult at the beginning to bring thoughts into captivity, but with diligence and patience it gets easier and swifter.

We need to discover our own type(s) of cages; we need to uncover what needs to be taken into captivity. What works for you may not work for someone else. Some people may use music that is filled with the word to uplift their spirit and keep their thoughts captive. Others might need to read the word. Even others may find praying and quoting scriptures a way for them to keep their thoughts captive. What really began working for me was writing down my thoughts and then searching the scripture to find examples where other people were delivered from the same or similar situations. For you it may be a combination of ways, but find your *cage* before the *box*.

Decide what type of cage you will build to house your thoughts. Will you give into unforgiveness, bitterness, and resentment? Will you succumb to jealousy, lying, backbiting? Will you build your mind with pornography and filth on social media, television and radio? Will you compromise and read the Bible only on Sunday. Will you go to church or spend Sunday morning sleeping in or attending a sporting event? Or will you give your mind over to Christ for complete control by filling it with only those things that are good and pure and Holy?

Getting into a box is rarely one dramatic moment: it's a process—a slow descent. In Scripture, people didn't usually fall all at once; they were drawn in step by step, like Jonah going "down to Joppa," then "down into the ship," and finally "down into the depths." In the same way, the boxes we find ourselves in are built and entered little by little—one thought, one wound, one compromise, one deception at a time. It isn't a single doorway but a series of smaller thresholds we cross almost without noticing. By the time the walls feel tight around us, we've already traveled deeper through many quiet steps.

When I began to understand that everyone's background and experiences shape how they think, feel, and act, I learned to extend more patience, compassion, and forgiveness. It's only through the love of Christ that I learned to walk in faith and peace—without judgment. Unforgiveness was the box that kept me trapped. Did anger fuel my depression, which in turn fed my pain and unhealthy coping mechanisms? Absolutely. Was I justified in feeling angry? I believed I was. But I wasn't justified to think others should feel what I felt. I wasn't justified to think that others had to respond and react the same way I did. Bible says, "Be angry and sin not" (Ephesians 4:6). I had allowed my anger to grow unchecked until it consumed me, pulling me into a painful, destructive cycle.

25 GROWING IN GRACE

Getting into a box is rarely one dramatic moment—it's a process, a slow descent. In Scripture, people didn't usually fall all at once; they were drawn in step by step, like Jonah going "down to Joppa," then "down into the ship," and finally "down into the depths." In the same way, the boxes we find ourselves in are built and entered little by little—one thought, one wound, one compromise, one deception at a time. It isn't a single doorway but a series of smaller thresholds we cross almost without noticing. By the time the walls feel tight around us, we've already traveled deeper through many quiet steps.

Adam and Eve remind us that decisions—even small ones—have ripples. God set a boundary for their protection, not their limitation. When they stepped outside of it and into the box, the consequences followed, not as punishment alone, but as a natural outcome of disobedience. The serpent didn't force them to eat; he planted doubt. Temptation often begins when we allow ourselves to question what we know is right, or when we entertain thoughts that pull us away from God's truth. Many things that look good, feel good, or promise something enticing aren't good for us. Even after their disobedience, God came walking through the garden asking where Adam was. God knew exactly where he was. His questioning came because He desired a relationship with Adam. This is the heart of God—He comes searching, even when we've fallen.

God made a promise to Abraham that he would have a child with his wife Sarah. When Sarah felt that God's promise of a child didn't come when she wanted it to, she convinced Abraham to have a child with Hagar. She and Abraham walked in a box—resulting in the birth of Ishmael—forcing Abraham to sink deeper in the box when he had to send Hagar and Ismael away. Even after all their mistakes, God still blessed Hagar and Ishmael and fulfilled His promises to Abraham and Sarah. God's love and purpose extend to all people, not just the ones chosen for a particular mission.

Joseph's brothers allowed jealousy to grow in their hearts. Even though Joseph's brothers sold him into slavery—pushing him into the box, God used that very situation to save nations from famine. What others intend for harm, God can transform for your benefit and His purpose. Sometimes the calling on your life attracts opposition, but it doesn't cancel the calling. In Pharaoh's palace, Joseph stayed faithful, honest, and hardworking—preparing him for elevation into greater places. Joseph spent years in situations that didn't match the promise God gave him. Joseph forgave his brothers—even after everything they did. Forgiveness does not excuse the wrong, but it sets you free and opens the door for healing and restoration.

Jeremiah obeyed God completely, yet, he was rejected by his family, beaten and imprisoned, and mocked by the nation. Life happened—surrounding Jeremiah in a box. His obedience puts him in direct conflict with the world around him. Faithfulness led to pain—not comfort. Jeremiah poured out his darkest emotions. He cried before

God; he questioned his existence, but God never scolded him. A true calling isn't always exciting or glamorous. Sometimes it feels heavy and costly. But what God places inside you will not let you be silent. By human standards, Jeremiah's ministry failed. But God did not measure him by results—only by obedience. Walking with God often means feeling what God feels—His burden for the lost, His grief over injustice, His compassion for the broken. Sometimes strength is simply staying where God put you, doing what He says, even when it hurts. Your darkest season may become someone else's greatest hope. When your life feels like ruins—God stands beside you. Even in suffering, nothing can separate you from His presence.

    I came from a tightly connected family. Our summers were spent on family vacations, road trips across the country, and Sundays meant Sunday school, dinner around the table, and Sunday night football. From an early age, certain truths were rooted in me: treat others as you would like to be treated, keep your promises, God is the same, yesterday, today, and tomorrow, and His rules are for our protection. And just as His guidance steadies us, we are called to adhere to the laws of man as unto God.

    Unkindness, deception, and betrayal approached me without warning—catching me unprepared for what I had never known. When faced with unkindness, I hid it within—confining me to a box of fear. When deception arose, I slipped further into the box. When betrayal surfaced, pushed deeper in the box, instead of rising up, I walked into the darkest depths of the box. I allowed unforgiveness, anger, and loathing to consume me—allowing depression to manifest—holding me hostage in the box, until I let go of the wheel and allow God to drive.

OUT OF THE BOX

Although what I believed to be my lowest point, actually became the beginning of my journey toward forgiveness and deliverance. What looked like an ending was, in truth, the start of my healing. That moment forced me to reach for the spiritual tools I had long abandoned—the ones that had been left to rust in the corner of my soul—the whole armor of God.

> **Put on the whole armor of God, that ye may be able to stand against the wiles of the devil. For we wrestle not against flesh and blood, but against principalities, against powers, against the rulers of the darkness of this world, against spiritual wickedness in high places. Wherefore take unto you the whole armor of God, that ye may be able to withstand in the evil day, and having done all, to stand. Stand therefore, having your loins girt about with truth, and having on the breastplate of righteousness; And your feet shod with the preparation of the gospel of peace; Above all, taking the shield of faith, wherewith ye shall be able to quench all the fiery darts of the wicked. And take the helmet of salvation, and the sword of the Spirit, which is the word of God: Praying always with all prayer and supplication in the Spirit, and watching thereunto with all perseverance and supplication for all saints. (Ephesians 6: 11- 18).**

Each piece of the armour became deeply personal to me—weapons I need to use to help me stand, when I felt to week to fight or move. I'd always known about the armour, but it means nothing to have armour and not use it. A soldier will not go to war without his armour.

He will not go to war with his helmet, but forget his boots. He will not omit to follow the order of his commanding officer.

When in battle, you need the *whole* armour. It's not enough to know the truth, but not live right. It's not enough to just pray and not walk in peace. It's not enough to have faith and not guard our mind. And it's not enough to live right when what we believe to be right does not line up with the Word of God.

The *Belt of Truth* helped me stay grounded in the truth of God's Word and rely on His strength rather than my own.

The *Breastplate of Righteousness* protected my heart by living in right relationship with God and choosing uprightness, even when it was hard.

The *Shoes of the Gospel of Peace* enabled me to walk in peace and be ready to share the message of hope and reconciliation wherever God leads me.

The *Shield of Faith* lifted my faith above my fears, trusting that it would extinguish every fiery dart of doubt, shame, and despair the enemy sends my way.

The *Helmet of Salvation* guarded my mind with the confidence that I am saved, chosen, and secure in Christ.

The *Sword of the Spirit* equipped me to wield God's Word as my weapon, speaking truth over lies and victory over defeat.

The final piece of armour, *Prayer,* kept me in constant communication with God—through every joy, every battle, and every moment of need.

Each time I reached for these spiritual tools, I felt a little stronger, a little freer, and a little closer to the woman God created me to be. Now, whenever a box tries to confine me again, I remember who I am, and to whom I belong and armor I prepare for battle. Does depression still try to creep in? Yes. Are there mornings when I have to pray for the strength just to get out of bed and face the day? Absolutely. Are there times when forgiveness is hard? Yes, but as our sins are forgiven, we must also forgive others—even when it's difficult. Forgiveness is not for the oppressor, but for the survivor. The difference today is that I allow the Greater One that lives within me to lead, guide, and protect me every step of the way—regardless. I remember my mom's favorite song, "It is Well with my Soul."

> *"When peace like a river attended my way, when sorrows like sea billows roll. Whatever my lot, Thou has taught me to say, it is well, it is well, with my soul."*

In the end, I stand as living proof that no box—no trial, no setback, no lie of the enemy—has the power to confine a child of God. Every barrier that once surrounded me, every limitation that tried to silence me, became the very ground on which I learned to fight. Not with my own strength, but clothed in the whole armor of God—His truth around my waist, His righteousness guarding my heart, His peace guiding my steps, His shield lifting me above the flames, His salvation covering my mind, and His Word lighting my path.

I walk forward delivered, restored, and set free. The boxes that once held me now testify of God's power to break chains I thought would last forever. And as I step into the fullness of who He created me to be, I carry a truth that no battle can shake and no darkness can steal:

It is well with my soul.

OUT OF THE BOX

www.ingramcontent.com/pod-product-compliance
Lightning Source LLC
Chambersburg PA
CBHW031417290426
44110CB00011B/416